FIRST ATLAS FOR CHILDREN

RING AROUND THE WORLD

A Wilco Book

Outstanding works of universal interest

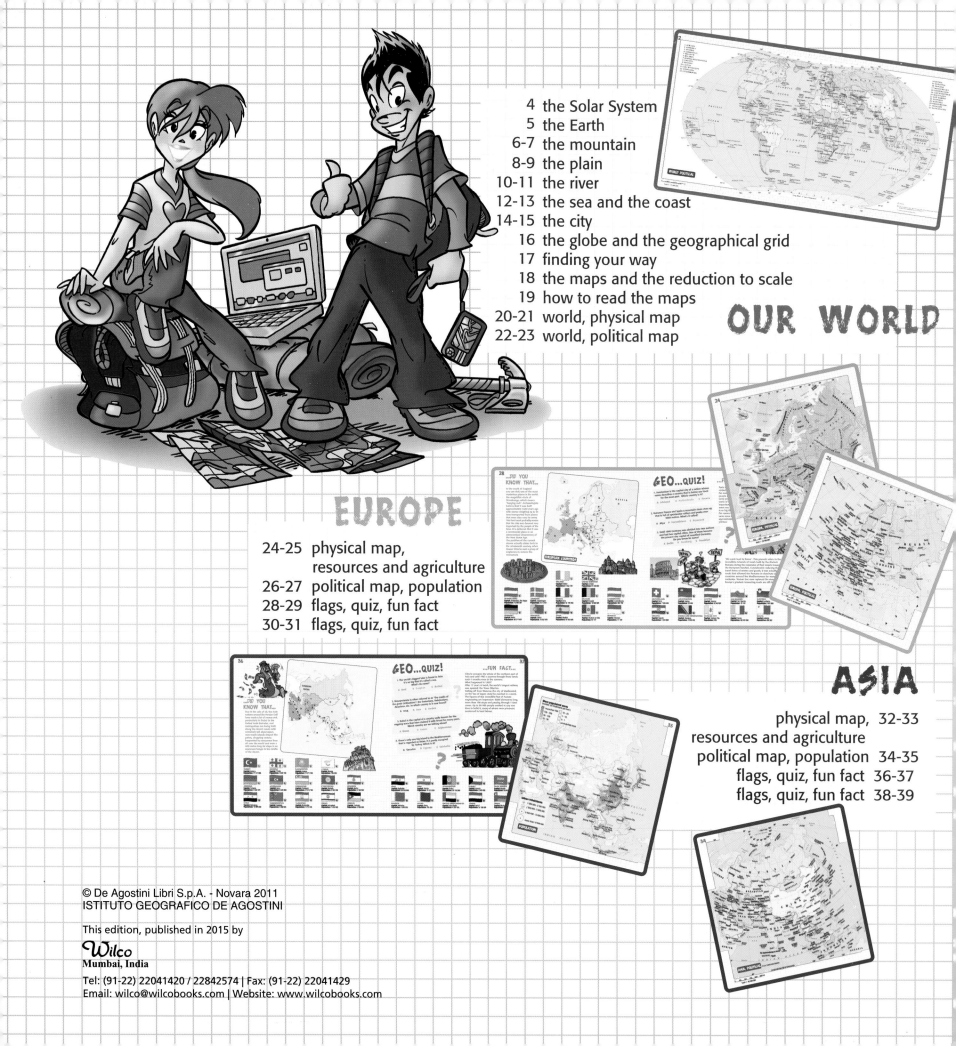

OUR WORLD

EUROPE

ASIA

© De Agostini Libri S.p.A. - Novara 2011
ISTITUTO GEOGRAFICO DE AGOSTINI

This edition, published in 2015 by

Wilco
Mumbai, India
Tel: (91-22) 22041420 / 22842574 | Fax: (91-22) 22041429
Email: wilco@wilcobooks.com | Website: www.wilcobooks.com

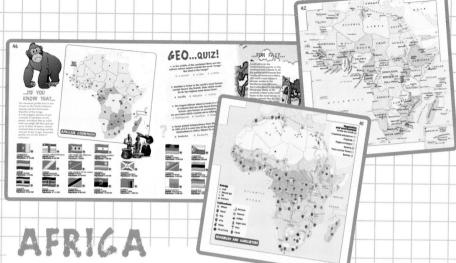

NORTH AMERICA

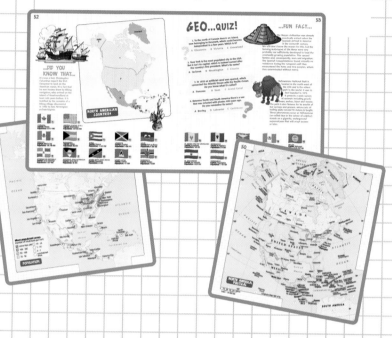

AFRICA

SOUTH AMERICA

OCEANIA AND POLES

INDEX OF NAMES

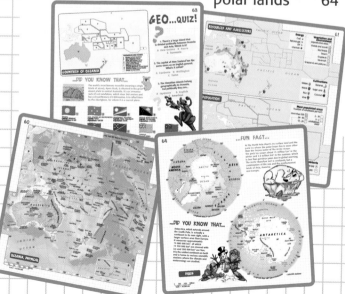

Maps included in this book are to be considered small graphical, symbolic and approximate representations of the Earth.

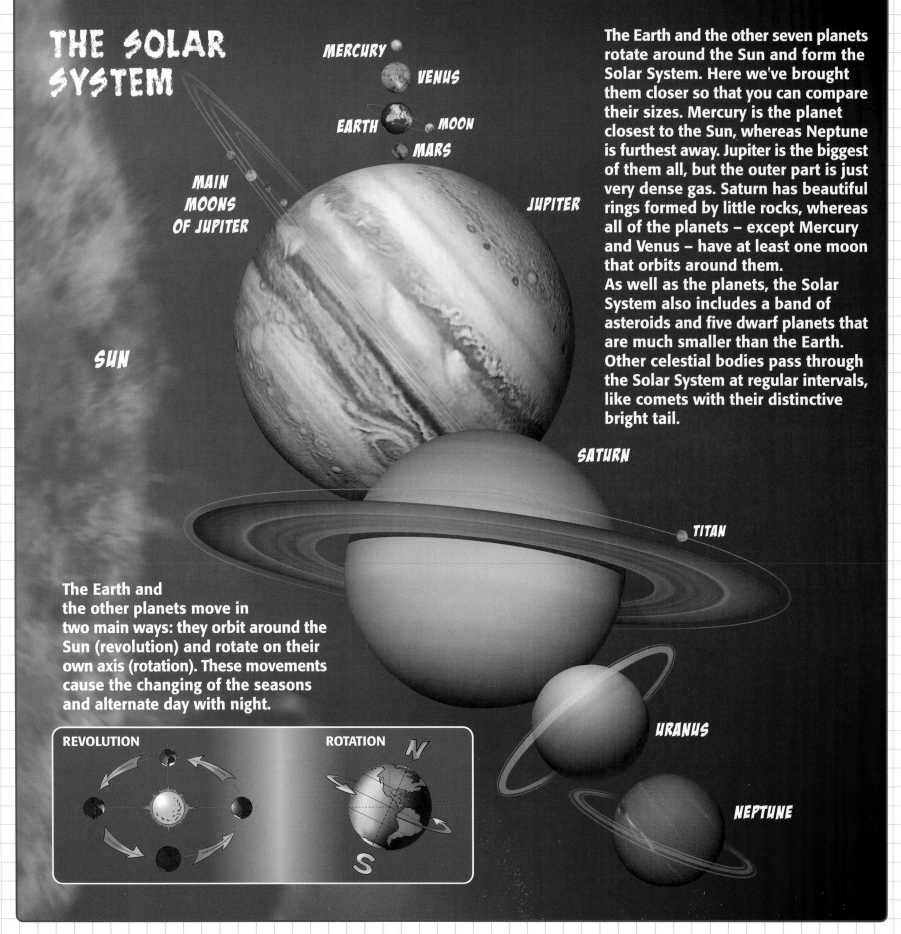

THE SOLAR SYSTEM

MERCURY

VENUS

EARTH — MOON

MARS

MAIN MOONS OF JUPITER

SUN

JUPITER

SATURN

TITAN

URANUS

NEPTUNE

The Earth and the other seven planets rotate around the Sun and form the Solar System. Here we've brought them closer so that you can compare their sizes. Mercury is the planet closest to the Sun, whereas Neptune is furthest away. Jupiter is the biggest of them all, but the outer part is just very dense gas. Saturn has beautiful rings formed by little rocks, whereas all of the planets – except Mercury and Venus – have at least one moon that orbits around them.

As well as the planets, the Solar System also includes a band of asteroids and five dwarf planets that are much smaller than the Earth. Other celestial bodies pass through the Solar System at regular intervals, like comets with their distinctive bright tail.

The Earth and the other planets move in two main ways: they orbit around the Sun (revolution) and rotate on their own axis (rotation). These movements cause the changing of the seasons and alternate day with night.

REVOLUTION

ROTATION

N

S

THE EARTH

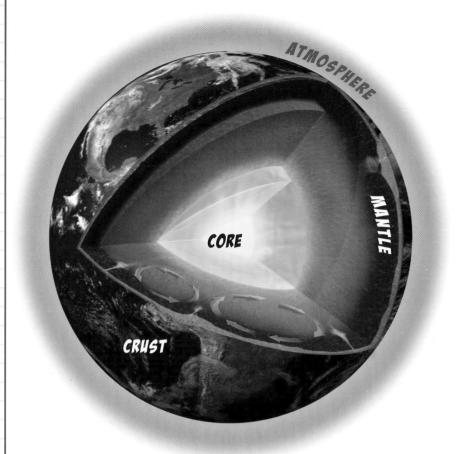

Our planet was formed four and a half billion years ago with the rest of the Solar System and was originally a ball of very hot matter. Over time the outer part (the *crust*) cooled and solidified, but it still conceals a red-hot mass of molten rock, called *magma,* divided into two layers, known as the *core* and *mantle.* We live on the crust in contact with the gaseous layer of air that surrounds the Earth, which is several kilometres thick and enables us to breathe. This shell is called the *atmosphere.*

The magma contained in the Earth arrives on the surface through volcanic eruptions. There are numerous volcanoes on our planet and they are formed by a passage that connects the underground tank of magma with the exit point called the crater. The crater is often at the top of a cone-shaped mountain formed by previous eruptions.

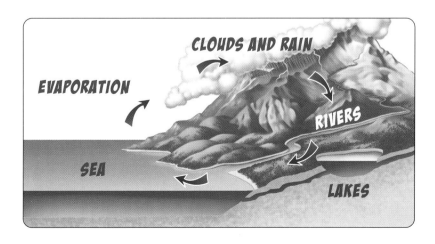

The land surface and the atmosphere are home to life on the Earth. The water cycle is one of the most important processes. The rain that falls from the sky feeds the rivers, fills the lakes and makes the soil fertile. Once it reaches the sea, through evaporation, the water returns to the sky to form the clouds that restart the cycle. The combination of all these elements make up the various environments of the Earth.

THE MOUNTAIN

The high grounds over 600 metres above sea level are called mountains. They form a very varied environment: the peaks are snow-capped all year round and are uninhabited.
The mountain slopes are home to shrubs at altitude and trees towards the valley. There are many wild animals, but it's hard to see them. Shepherds live with their animals in the pastures, whereas the valley floor is occupied by roads and villages.

PASS

MASSIF

PLATEAU

TUNNEL

VALLEY

TRAIL

PASTURE

SUMMIT OR PEAK

GLACIER

AVALANCHE

SKI SLOPES

VALLEY

THE PLAIN

IRRIGATION CANAL

FARMED FIELDS

RICE FIELD

HAY

SPRING

POND

The flat area between sea level and 200-300 metres of altitude is known as the plain. It is the place that lends itself best to the development of farming, roads and towns. In the past the plains were covered with forests and populated by many animals. Nowadays, most of the woodland has been cleared to make way for agriculture and wild vegetation can only really be seen along the rivers and in nature parks.

FARM

RIVER

THE RIVER

SOURCE

RAIN

RIVULET

WATERFALL

NATURAL LAKE

BRIDGE

CANAL

The river is a perennial waterway, meaning that it maintains a fairly constant flow all year round. Its source is usually in the mountains and it's fed by the melting of snow and ice. Waterfalls are found along the rivers at sudden differences in height and lakes when the water meets a depression. Man creates reservoirs to produce electricity through the construction of dams.

THE SEA AND THE COAST

LIGHTHOUSE

HEADLAND

ISLAND

BAY

ISTHMUS

CLIFF

STRAIT

LOW-LYING COAST

DELTA

RIVER

The sea occupies almost three-quarters of the Earth's surface, so it influences the climate. Man crosses it mainly to transport goods from one end of the Earth to the other. Along the coast, man has created great cities and enormous ports, where ships and fishing boats set sail. The seas in hot and temperate areas welcome millions of tourists every year who frequent the beaches and marinas, where sailing boats and cruise ships set sail.

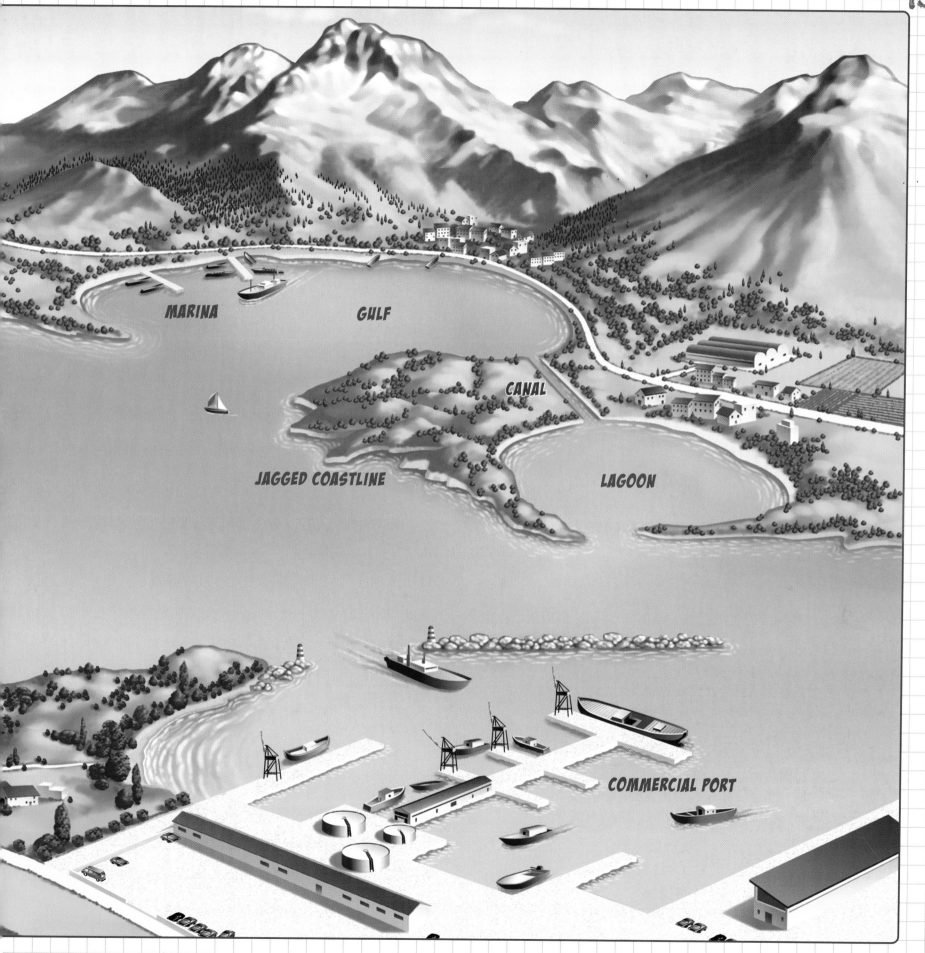

MARINA

GULF

CANAL

JAGGED COASTLINE

LAGOON

COMMERCIAL PORT

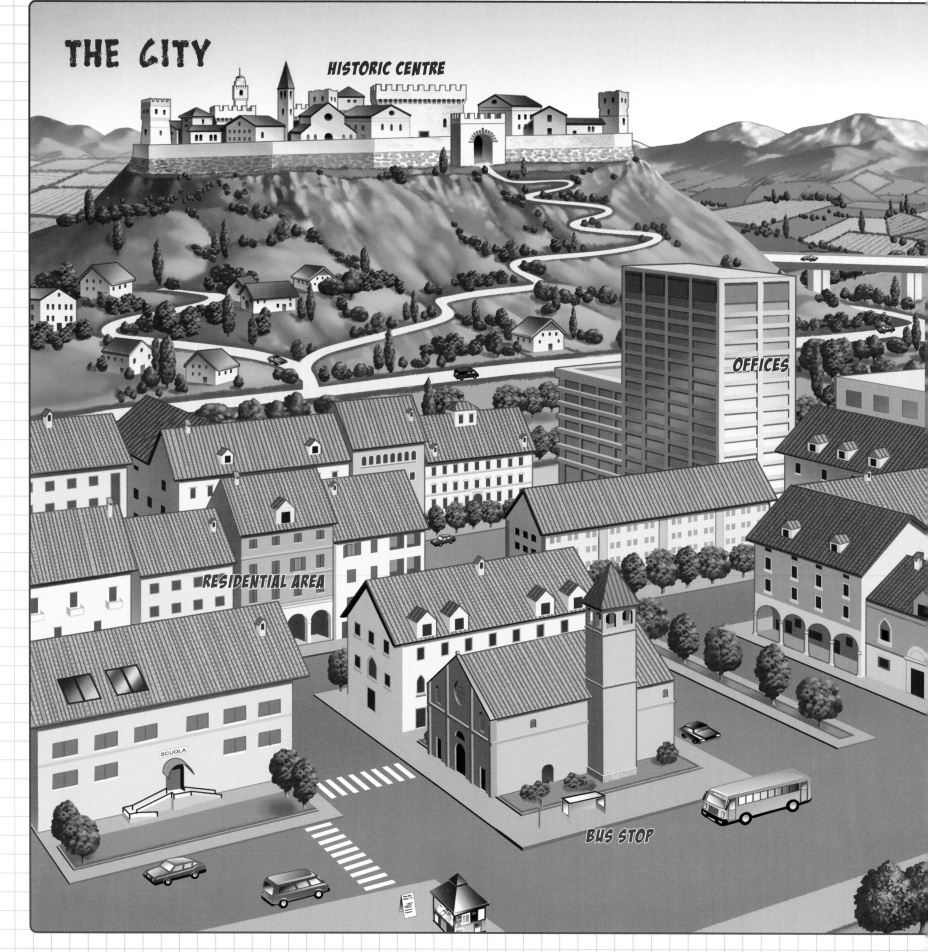

THE CITY

HISTORIC CENTRE

OFFICES

RESIDENTIAL AREA

SCUOLA

BUS STOP

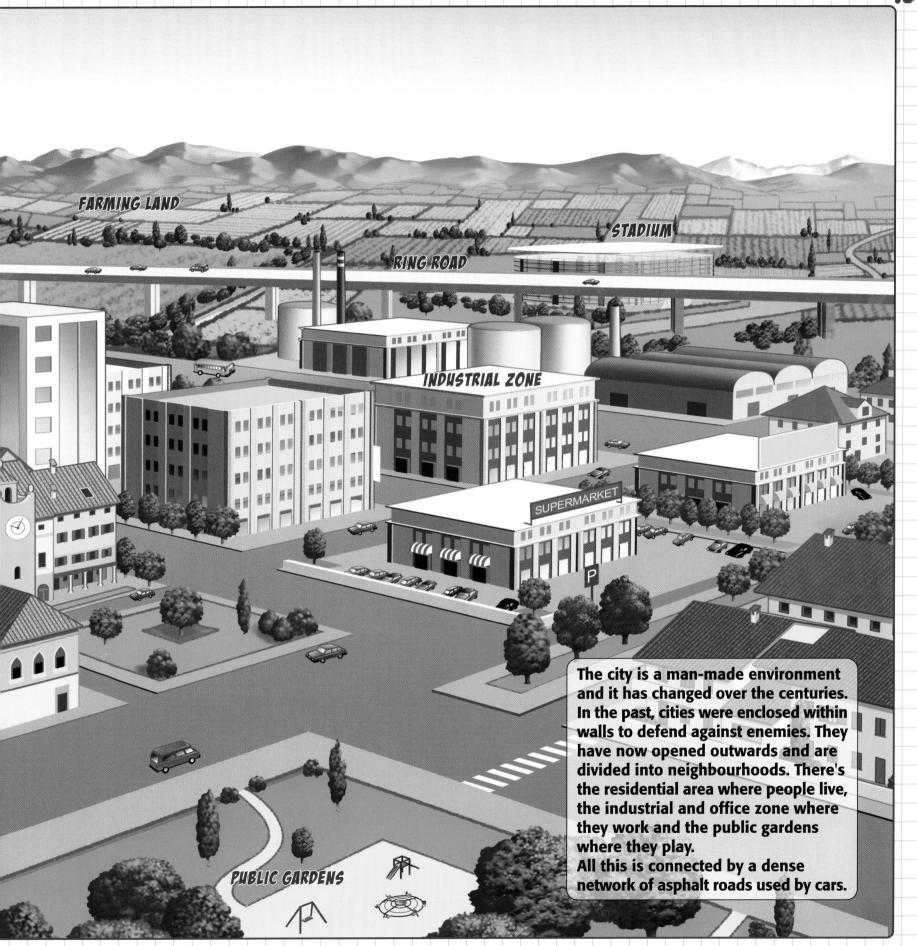

FARMING LAND

STADIUM

RING ROAD

INDUSTRIAL ZONE

SUPERMARKET

P

PUBLIC GARDENS

The city is a man-made environment and it has changed over the centuries. In the past, cities were enclosed within walls to defend against enemies. They have now opened outwards and are divided into neighbourhoods. There's the residential area where people live, the industrial and office zone where they work and the public gardens where they play.
All this is connected by a dense network of asphalt roads used by cars.

GLOBE AND THE GEOGRAPHICAL GRID

The planet on which we live, the Earth, is shaped like a sphere and man has had to invent a way to identify the position of any given place on it. In order to make this atlas and to draw up all the maps in it, the cartographers divided up the Earth's surface with a series of criss-crossing horizontal and vertical lines, forming an invisible grid known as the *geographical grid*.
The vertical lines, the ones that join together the two poles, are the *meridians* (or *lines of longitude)*, whereas the horizontal lines form parallel circumferences, known as *parallels* (or *lines of latitude).*

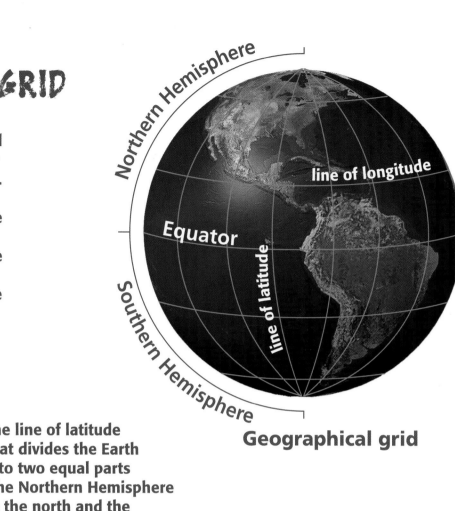

Geographical grid

The line of latitude that divides the Earth into two equal parts (the Northern Hemisphere to the north and the Southern Hemisphere to the south) is called the *Equator.*

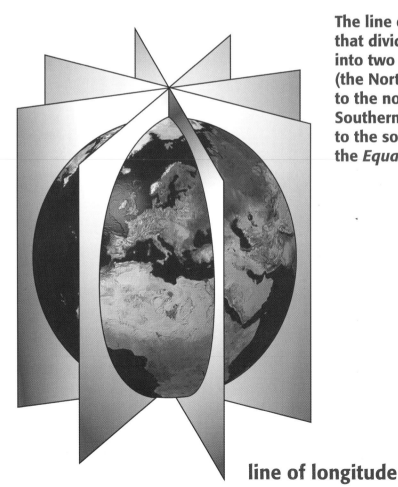

line of longitude

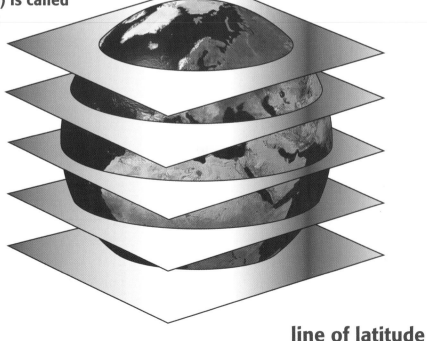

line of latitude

FINDING YOUR WAY

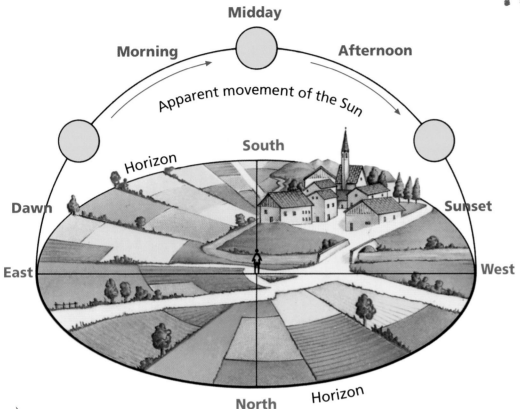

Before learning how to read the maps, you need to know how to find your way in day-to-day life. There are now modern tools available like sat navs, but you need to know the basic rules of orientation to know how to use them well.

First of all, the compass with its points is the oldest tool that lets us find where we are.

The compass is similar to a clock face, but in place of the hands it has a magnetic needle that always points to the north.

The compass is therefore a safe reference, but there are also other methods of finding your way.

Every day the Sun completes the same path in the sky: it rises in the east and sets in the west, passing the south at exactly midday. At that moment, if you position yourself with your face pointing towards the Sun and stretch your arms out, you'll have the east to your left and west to your right.

If there are no clouds and you've got a watch with hands available, you can also find your way fairly easily at a different time of day.

Let's try it. Point the hour hand towards the Sun and trace an imaginary line that runs halfway between the hour hand and the notch that marks the 12 on the clock face: that line shows you where south is. Now that you know the basic rules of orientation, you can help your mum or dad to program the sat nav!

THE MAPS AND REDUCTION TO SCALE

Having established the geographical grid, the cartographer has to decide the *scale* of the map he/she wants to draw up.

The scale indicates how many times the objects shown on the map have been reduced by compared with the real items. The scale is shown using two numbers. The first is always 1 and represents the actual measurement, whereas the second number establishes by how many times the things have been reduced. E.g. When you see *scale 1 : 1000* written on maps, it reads as *one to one thousand* and means that all the real objects have been reduced by 1000 times. Next to this wording, you can often find a small bar divided into segments that show the actual measurements. So, in our example, 1 centimetre on the bar corresponds to 1000 centimetres in real life, that is 10 metres.

Is that too hard? Don't worry. With time and a few simple exercises, you'll easily learn how to use the scale. Look at the example below. We chose an item that you know well: a pencil sharpener. The first drawing shows it at the size it actually is. From the second drawing onwards, it is reduced and the scale shows by how much.

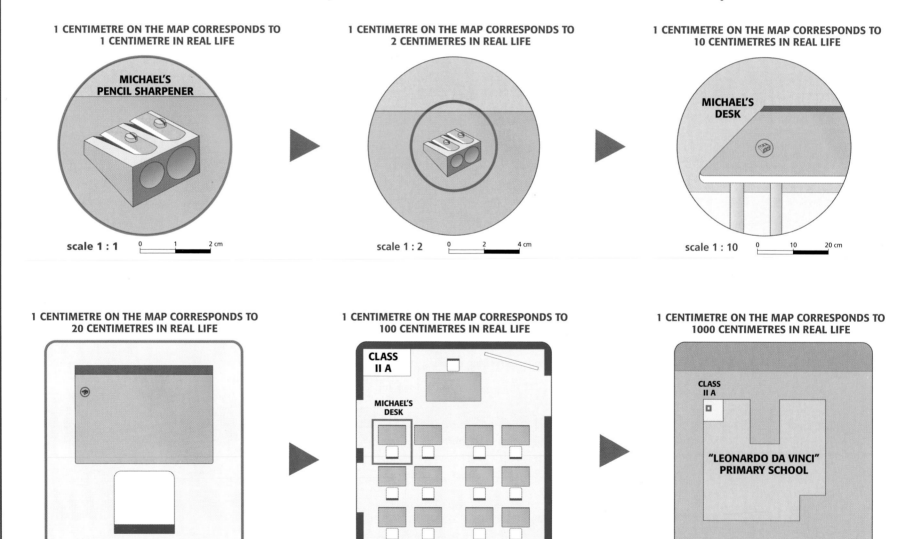

1 CENTIMETRE ON THE MAP CORRESPONDS TO 1 CENTIMETRE IN REAL LIFE

MICHAEL'S PENCIL SHARPENER

scale 1 : 1   0   1   2 cm

1 CENTIMETRE ON THE MAP CORRESPONDS TO 2 CENTIMETRES IN REAL LIFE

scale 1 : 2   0   2   4 cm

1 CENTIMETRE ON THE MAP CORRESPONDS TO 10 CENTIMETRES IN REAL LIFE

MICHAEL'S DESK

scale 1 : 10   0   10   20 cm

1 CENTIMETRE ON THE MAP CORRESPONDS TO 20 CENTIMETRES IN REAL LIFE

scale 1 : 20   0   20   40 cm

1 CENTIMETRE ON THE MAP CORRESPONDS TO 100 CENTIMETRES IN REAL LIFE

CLASS II A

MICHAEL'S DESK

scale 1 : 100   0   1   2 m

1 CENTIMETRE ON THE MAP CORRESPONDS TO 1000 CENTIMETRES IN REAL LIFE

CLASS II A

"LEONARDO DA VINCI" PRIMARY SCHOOL

scale 1 : 1000   0   10   20 m

HOW TO READ THE MAPS

You've learnt that maps are a reduced representation of real life, but they are much more besides!
They are also *approximate,* meaning that they are as similar as possible, but are not the same as real life. They are also *symbolic,* that is they use symbols that everyone can understand to represent particular objects.

For example, cities are small circles, borders are lines and mountain peaks are little dots or triangles. On this page you'll find the *key,* which explains the symbols you'll find on the political and physical maps. There are also *thematic* maps, which deal with particular themes and usually have a special key.

POLITICAL MAP

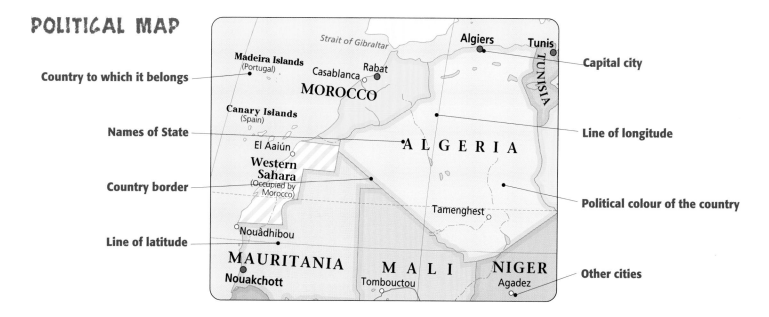

Country to which it belongs
Names of State
Country border
Line of latitude

Capital city
Line of longitude
Political colour of the country
Other cities

PHYSICAL MAP

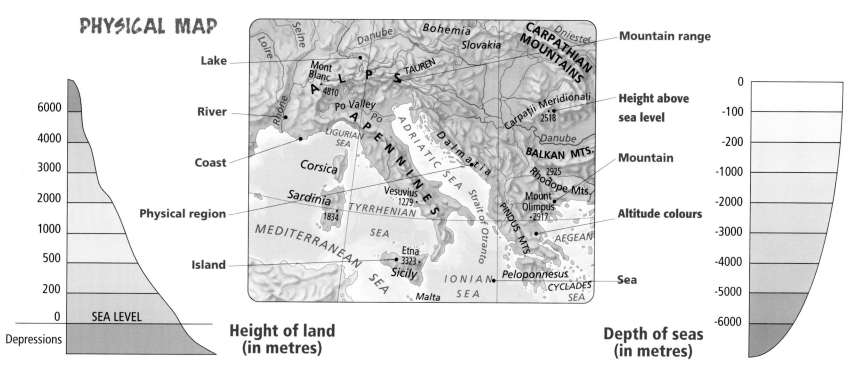

Lake
River
Coast
Physical region
Island

Mountain range
Height above sea level
Mountain
Altitude colours
Sea

6000
4000
3000
2000
1000
500
200
0 SEA LEVEL
Depressions

Height of land (in metres)

0
-100
-200
-1000
-2000
-3000
-4000
-5000
-6000

Depth of seas (in metres)

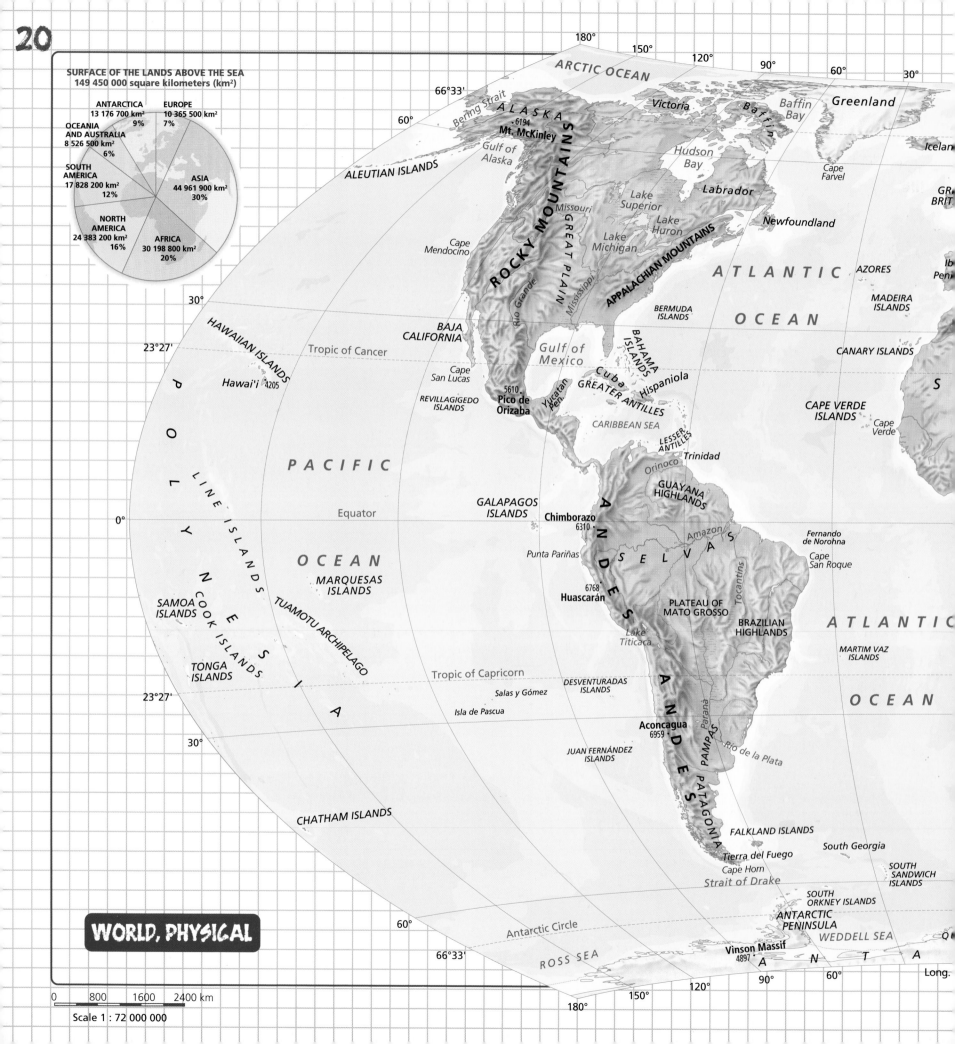

SURFACE OF THE LANDS ABOVE THE SEA
149 450 000 square kilometers (km²)

ANTARCTICA
13 176 700 km²
9%

EUROPE
10 365 500 km²
7%

OCEANIA
AND AUSTRALIA
8 526 500 km²
6%

ASIA
44 961 900 km²
30%

SOUTH
AMERICA
17 828 200 km²
12%

NORTH
AMERICA
24 383 200 km²
16%

AFRICA
30 198 800 km²
20%

ARCTIC OCEAN

66°33'

180°
150°
120°
90°
60°
30°

Greenland

Victoria

Baffin

Baffin
Bay

Icelan

60°

ALASKA
6194
Mt. McKinley

Gulf of
Alaska

Hudson
Bay

Labrador

Cape
Farvel

GR
BRIT

ALEUTIAN ISLANDS

Bering Strait

ROCKY MOUNTAINS

GREAT PLAIN

Missouri

Lake
Superior

Lake
Michigan

Lake
Huron

APPALACHIAN MOUNTAINS

Newfoundland

ATLANTIC

AZORES

OCEAN

Ib
Pen

30°

Cape
Mendocino

Rio Grande

Mississippi

BERMUDA
ISLANDS

MADEIRA
ISLANDS

HAWAIIAN ISLANDS

BAJA
CALIFORNIA

Gulf of
Mexico

BAHAMA
ISLANDS

Cuba
GREATER ANTILLES

Hispaniola

CANARY ISLANDS

23°27'
Tropic of Cancer

Hawai'i 4205

Cape
San Lucas

5610
Pico de
Orizaba

Yucatan
Pen.

CARIBBEAN SEA

CAPE VERDE
ISLANDS

Cape
Verde

REVILLAGIGEDO
ISLANDS

LESSER
ANTILLES

Trinidad

P

PACIFIC

O

Orinoco

GUAYANA
HIGHLANDS

GALAPAGOS
ISLANDS

Chimborazo
6310

Amazon

Fernando
de Norohna

0°
Equator

L

ANDES

SELVAS

Cape
San Roque

Y

OCEAN

Punta Pariñas

N

MARQUESAS
ISLANDS

6768
Huascarán

Tocantins

PLATEAU OF
MATO GROSSO

ATLANTIC

E

BRAZILIAN
HIGHLANDS

SAMOA
ISLANDS

COOK ISLANDS

S

Lake
Titicaca

LINE ISLANDS

I

MARTIM VAZ
ISLANDS

TONGA
ISLANDS

A

TUAMOTU ARCHIPELAGO

Tropic of Capricorn

23°27'

Salas y Gómez

DESVENTURADAS
ISLANDS

ANDES

OCEAN

Isla de Pascua

Paraná

30°

JUAN FERNÁNDEZ
ISLANDS

Aconcagua
6959

PAMPAS

Río de la Plata

CHATHAM ISLANDS

PATAGONIA

FALKLAND ISLANDS

South Georgia

60°

Tierra del Fuego
Cape Horn
Strait of Drake

SOUTH
SANDWICH
ISLANDS

SOUTH
ORKNEY ISLANDS

Antarctic Circle

ANTARCTIC
PENINSULA

WEDDELL SEA

66°33'

ROSS SEA

Vinson Massif
4897

A

N

T

A

Long.

180°

150°

120°

90°

60°

0   800   1600   2400 km

Scale 1 : 72 000 000

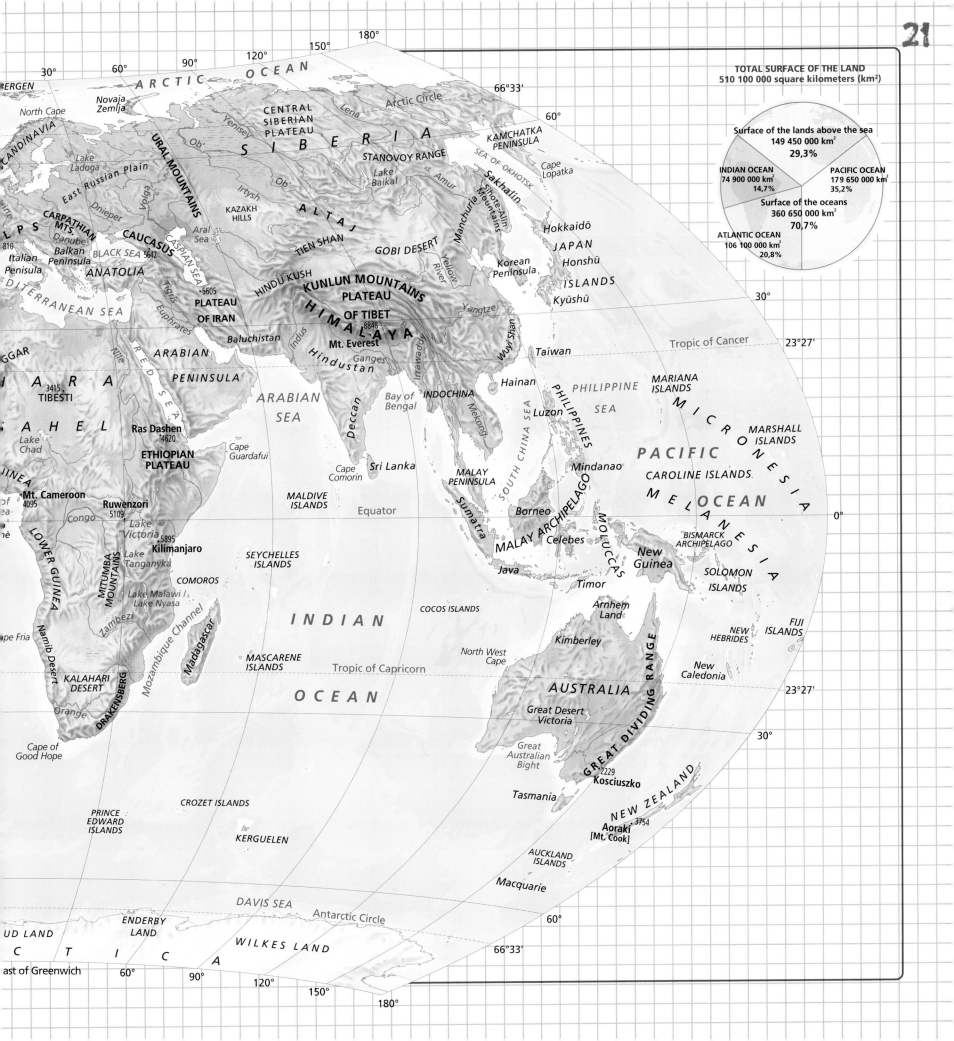

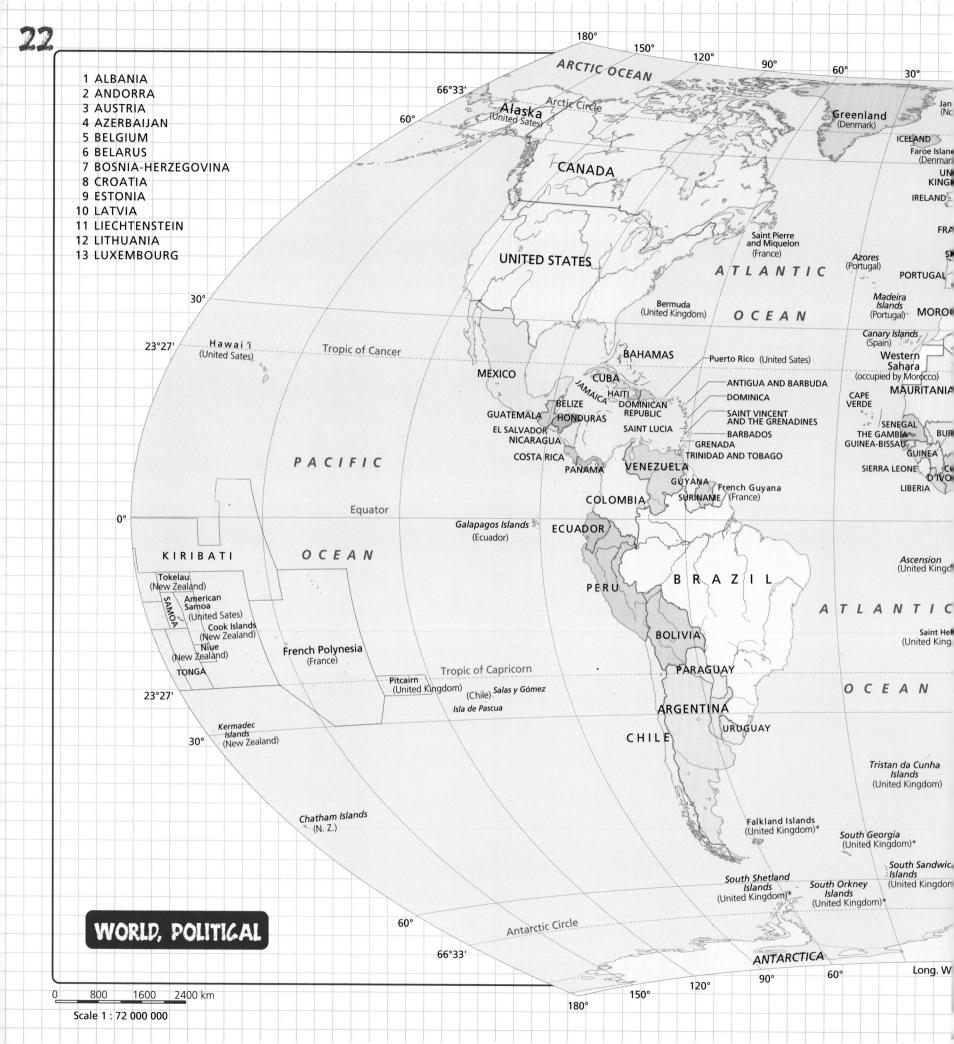

22

WORLD, POLITICAL

1 ALBANIA
2 ANDORRA
3 AUSTRIA
4 AZERBAIJAN
5 BELGIUM
6 BELARUS
7 BOSNIA-HERZEGOVINA
8 CROATIA
9 ESTONIA
10 LATVIA
11 LIECHTENSTEIN
12 LITHUANIA
13 LUXEMBOURG

ARCTIC OCEAN

180°   150°   120°   90°   60°   30°

66°33'   Arctic Circle

Greenland
(Denmark)

Jan (No

Alaska
(United Sates)

ICELAND

Faroe Islan
(Denma

CANADA

UN
KING

IRELAND

60°

UNITED STATES

ATLANTIC

FRA

Saint Pierre
and Miquelon
(France)

Azores
(Portugal)

S

30°

OCEAN

PORTUGAL

Bermuda
(United Kingdom)

Madeira
Islands
(Portugal)

MORO

23°27'   Tropic of Cancer

Hawai'i
(United Sates)

Canary Islands
(Spain)

Western
Sahara
(occupied by Morocco)

BAHAMAS

Puerto Rico (United Sates)

MEXICO   CUBA

MAURITANIA

JAMAICA   HAITI

ANTIGUA AND BARBUDA

CAPE
VERDE

BELIZE   DOMINICAN
REPUBLIC

DOMINICA

GUATEMALA   HONDURAS

SAINT VINCENT
AND THE GRENADINES

SENEGAL

EL SALVADOR   SAINT LUCIA

THE GAMBIA

BUR

NICARAGUA

BARBADOS

GUINEA-BISSAU

PACIFIC

COSTA RICA

GRENADA

GUINEA

PANAMA   VENEZUELA

TRINIDAD AND TOBAGO

SIERRA LEONE

D'IVO

GUYANA

Equator

COLOMBIA

SURINAME

French Guyana
(France)

LIBERIA

0°

Galapagos Islands
(Ecuador)

ECUADOR

KIRIBATI

OCEAN

Tokelau
(New Zealand)

PERU

B R A Z I L

ATLANTIC

American
Samoa
(United Sates)

SAMOA

Cook Islands
(New Zealand)

Ascension
(United Kingo

Niue
(New Zealand)

French Polynesia
(France)

BOLIVIA

Saint He
(United King

TONGA

PARAGUAY

OCEAN

23°27'   Tropic of Capricorn

Pitcairn
(United Kingdom)

(Chile) Salas y Gómez

Isla de Pascua

ARGENTINA

30°

Kermadec
Islands
(New Zealand)

URUGUAY

CHILE

Chatham Islands
(N. Z.)

Tristan da Cunha
Islands
(United Kingdom)

Falkland Islands
(United Kingdom)*

South Georgia
(United Kingdom)*

South Sandwic
Islands
(United Kingdom)

South Shetland
Islands
(United Kingdom)*

South Orkney
Islands
(United Kingdom)*

66°33'

Antarctic Circle

ANTARCTICA   Long. W

120°   90°   60°

150°

180°

WORLD, POLITICAL

0   800   1600   2400 km

Scale 1 : 72 000 000

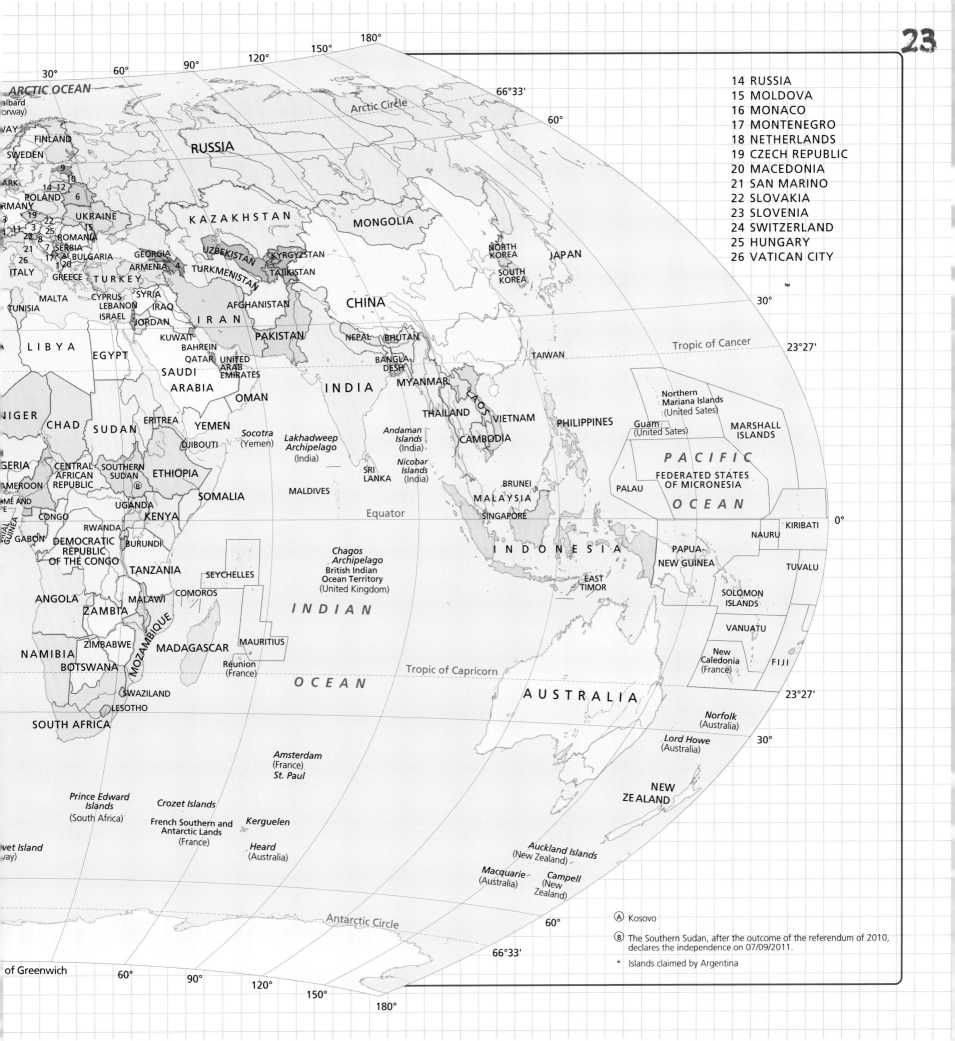

14 RUSSIA
15 MOLDOVA
16 MONACO
17 MONTENEGRO
18 NETHERLANDS
19 CZECH REPUBLIC
20 MACEDONIA
21 SAN MARINO
22 SLOVAKIA
23 SLOVENIA
24 SWITZERLAND
25 HUNGARY
26 VATICAN CITY

ARCTIC OCEAN
albard
orway)

NAY
FINLAND
SWEDEN
ARK
DARK
GERMANY
POLAND 6
19 22 UKRAINE
11 3 25
23 8 7 ROMANIA
21 SERBIA
26 17 A BULGARIA
ITALY 1 20
GREECE TURKEY
TUNISIA MALTA
CYPRUS SYRIA
LEBANON IRAQ
ISRAEL JORDAN
LIBYA EGYPT

RUSSIA

KAZAKHSTAN

MONGOLIA

GEORGIA
ARMENIA 4
UZBEKISTAN KYRGYZSTAN
TURKMENISTAN TAJIKISTAN
AFGHANISTAN
IRAN
PAKISTAN
CHINA

NORTH
KOREA
SOUTH
KOREA
JAPAN

Arctic Circle
66°33'
60°

30°

Tropic of Cancer   23°27'

KUWAIT
BAHREIN
QATAR
UNITED
ARAB
EMIRATES
SAUDI
ARABIA
OMAN
YEMEN

NEPAL BHUTAN
BANGLA-
DESH
INDIA
MYANMAR
THAILAND LAOS
VIETNAM
CAMBODIA

TAIWAN

PHILIPPINES

Northern
Mariana Islands
(United Sates)
Guam
(United Sates)

MARSHALL
ISLANDS

PACIFIC

NIGER
CHAD SUDAN
ERITREA
DJIBOUTI
CENTRAL
AFRICAN SOUTHERN
REPUBLIC SUDAN
ETHIOPIA
SOMALIA

Socotra
(Yemen)
Lakhadweep
Archipelago
(India)

Andaman
Islands
(India)

SRI
LANKA
Nicobar
Islands
(India)
MALDIVES

BRUNEI

PALAU

FEDERATED STATES
OF MICRONESIA

OCEAN

ERIA
AMEROON
MÉ AND
GUINEA
CONGO
GABON
DEMOCRATIC
REPUBLIC
OF THE CONGO

RWANDA
BURUNDI
UGANDA
KENYA
TANZANIA

SEYCHELLES

Chagos
Archipelago
British Indian
Ocean Territory
(United Kingdom)

MALAYSIA
SINGAPORE

INDONESIA

EAST
TIMOR

Equator

PAPUA-
NEW GUINEA

NAURU KIRIBATI   0°

TUVALU

ANGOLA
ZAMBIA
NAMIBIA
BOTSWANA
ZIMBABWE
MOZAMBIQUE
SWAZILAND
LESOTHO
SOUTH AFRICA

MALAWI
COMOROS
MADAGASCAR
MAURITIUS
Réunion
(France)

INDIAN

OCEAN

SOLOMON
ISLANDS

VANUATU

New
Caledonia
(France)

FIJI

Tropic of Capricorn   23°27'

AUSTRALIA

Norfolk
(Australia)

30°

Lord Howe
(Australia)

Amsterdam
(France)
St. Paul

Prince Edward
Islands
(South Africa)

Crozet Islands

French Southern and
Antarctic Lands
(France)

Kerguelen

Heard
(Australia)

Auckland Islands
(New Zealand)

NEW
ZEALAND

vet Island
vay)

Macquarie
(Australia)

Campell
(New
Zealand)

Antarctic Circle

60°

Ⓐ Kosovo

Ⓑ The Southern Sudan, after the outcome of the referendum of 2010,
declares the independence on 07/09/2011.

* Islands claimed by Argentina

66°33'

of Greenwich   60°   90°

120°

150°

180°

30° 60° 90° 120° 150° 180°

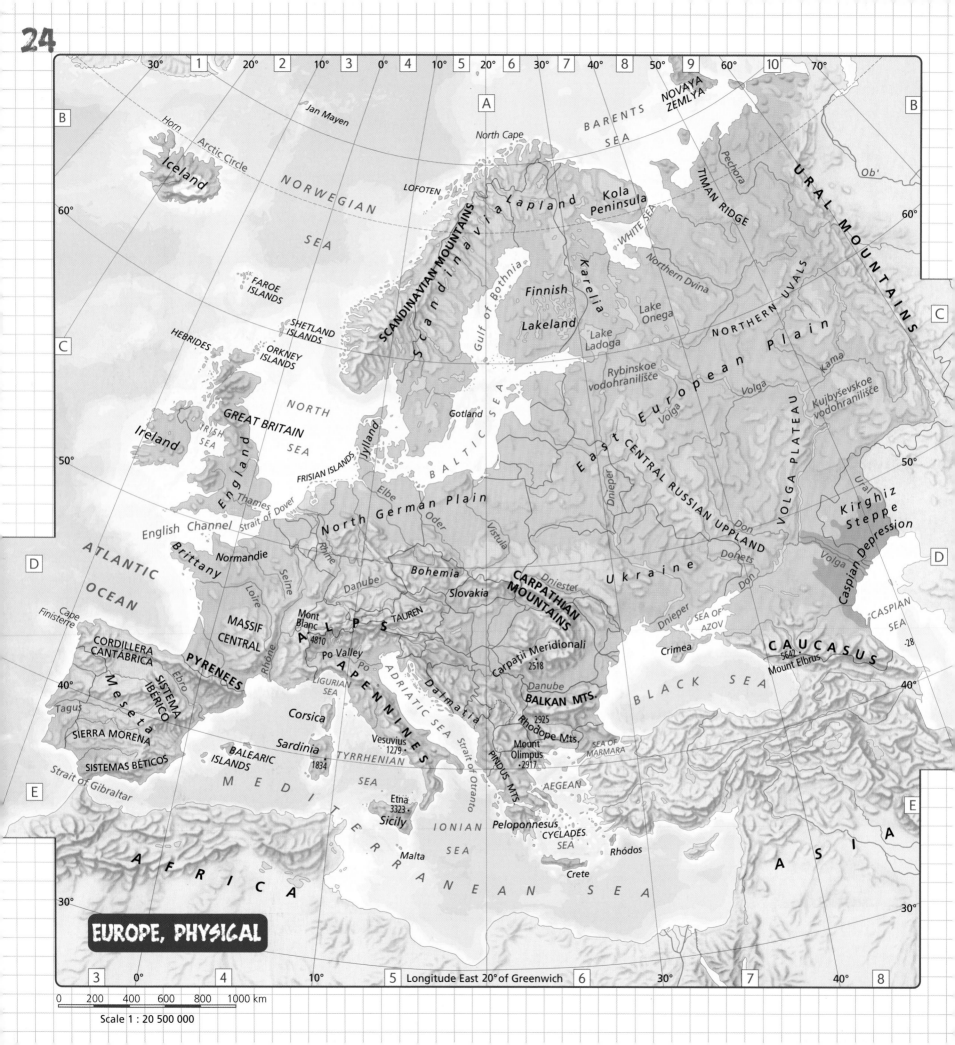

24

EUROPE, PHYSICAL

Scale 1 : 20 500 000

0 200 400 600 800 1000 km

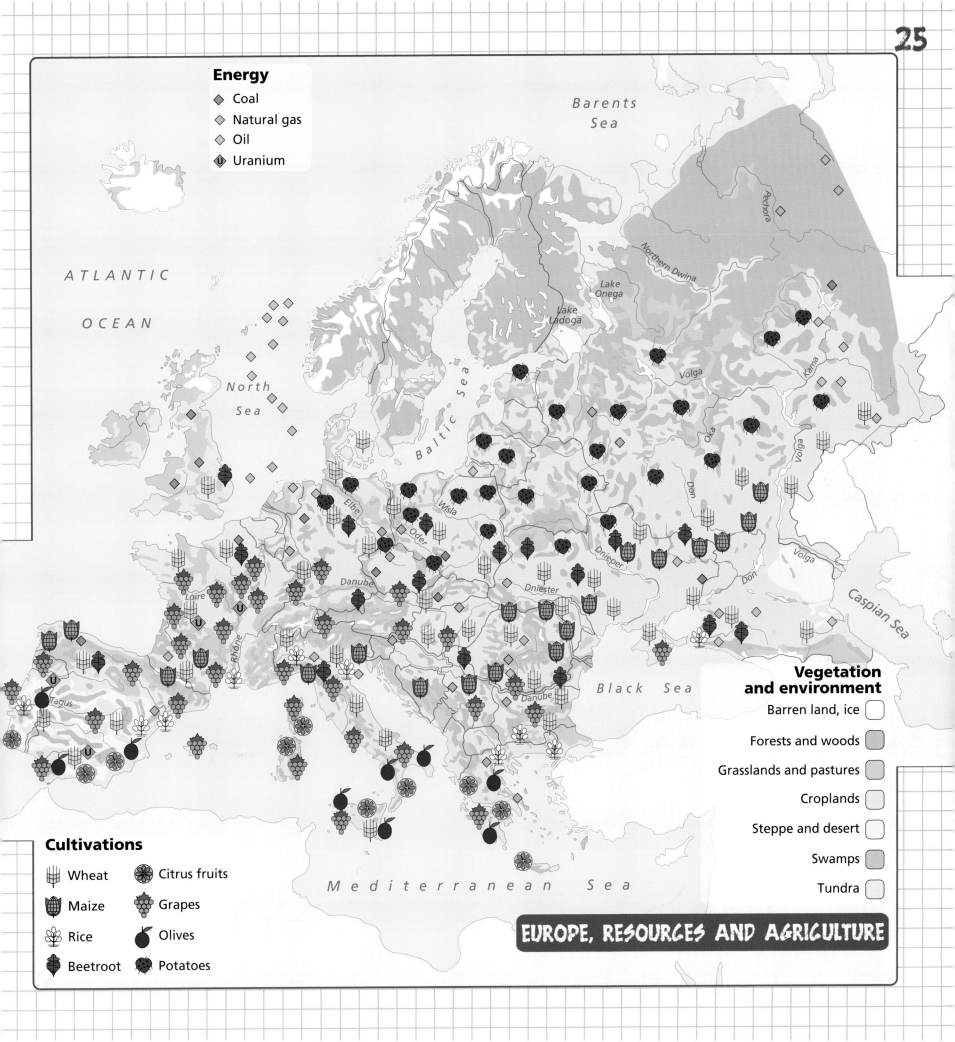

Energy

◆ Coal
◇ Natural gas
◇ Oil
Ⓤ Uranium

Barents Sea

ATLANTIC OCEAN

North Sea

Baltic Sea

Pechora

Northern Dwina

Lake Onega

Lake Ladoga

Volga

Oka

Kama

Elbe

Wisla

Don

Volga

Oder

Loire

Rhône

Danube

Dnieper

Dniester

Don

Volga

Caspian Sea

Tagus

Danube

Black Sea

Vegetation and environment

Barren land, ice ☐
Forests and woods ☐
Grasslands and pastures ☐
Croplands ☐
Steppe and desert ☐
Swamps ☐
Tundra ☐

Mediterranean Sea

Cultivations

🌾 Wheat
🌽 Maize
🌱 Rice
🌰 Beetroot
❀ Citrus fruits
🍇 Grapes
🫒 Olives
🥔 Potatoes

EUROPE, RESOURCES AND AGRICULTURE

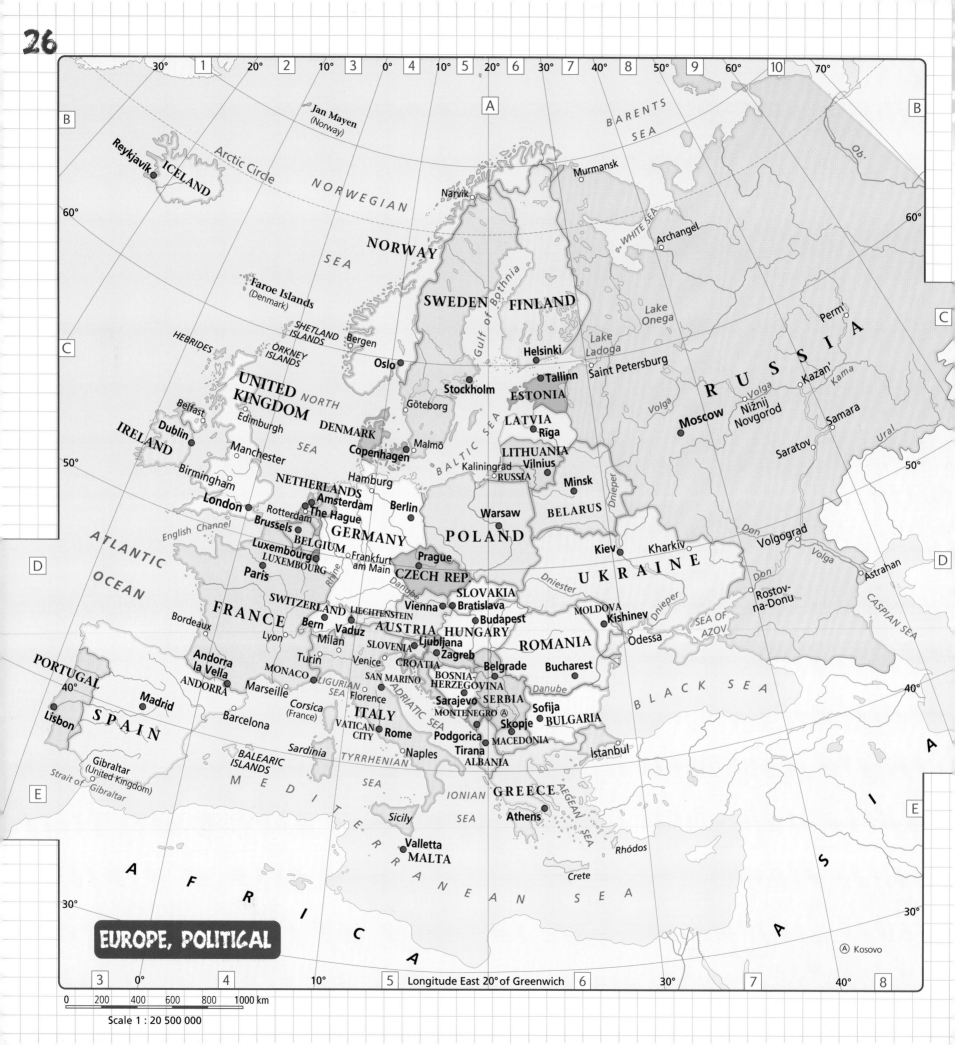

EUROPE, POLITICAL

26

Scale 1 : 20 500 000

| 0 | 200 | 400 | 600 | 800 | 1000 km |

Longitude East 20° of Greenwich

Barents Sea

ATLANTIC OCEAN

North Sea

Baltico Sea

Perm'

Stockholm

Saint Petersburg

Kazan'

Dublin

Copenhagen

Moscow

Nižnij Novgorod

Samara

Manchester

Hamburg

Minsk

Amsterdam

Berlin

Warsaw

Volgograd

London

Rotterdam

Brussels

Kiev

Rostov-na-Donu

Paris

Prague

Caspian Sea

München

Vienna

Budapest

Lyon

Odessa

Milan

Bucharest

Black Sea

Lisbon

Belgrade

Madrid

Marseille

Barcelona

Sofia

Rome

Naples

Athens

Mediterranean Sea

Most populated areas

(number of inhabitants per km²)

0 - 10		100 - 200	
10 - 50		200 - 500	
50 - 100		more than 500	

EUROPE, POPULATION

Urban inhabitants

1 000 000 - 2 500 000

2 500 000 - 5 000 000

5 000 000 - 10 000 000

more than 10 000 000

...DID YOU KNOW THAT...

In the south of England you can visit one of the most mysterious places in the world: the megalithic circle of Stonehenge, which means "hanging rock". Archaeologists believe that it was built approximately 4500 years ago with stones weighing up to 50 tons transported from places that were also very far away. This hard work probably means that the site was deemed very important by the people of the time. It is believed that it was a ceremonial place or an astronomical observatory of the New Stone Age.
The position of the current stones actually dates back to the nineteenth century, when Queen Victoria sent a group of engineers to restore the monument

EUROPEAN COUNTRIES

IRELAND
Capital: Dublin
Population: 4 422 100

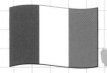

UNITED KINGDOM
Capital: London
Population: 61 446 000

NETHERLANDS
Capital: Amsterdam
Population: 16 486 587

DENMARK
Capital: Copenhagen
Population: 5 511 451

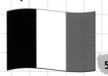

FRANCE
Capital: Paris
Population: 62 106 000

BELGIUM
Capital: Brussels
Population: 10 666 866

LUXEMBOURG
Capital: Luxembourg
Population: 483 799

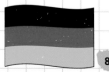

GERMANY
Capital: Berlin
Population: 82 217 837

PORTUGAL
Capital: Lisbon
Population: 10 627 000

SPAIN
Capital: Madrid
Population: 45 453 685

ANDORRA
Capital: Andorra la Vella
Population: 83 137

MONACO
Capital: Monaco
Population: 31 109

GEO...QUIZ!

1. Amsterdam is the capital city of a nation whose name describes a country that is below sea level for the most part. Which country is it?

A Irleland   B Netherlands   C France

2. Between France and Spain a mountain chain rises up that is full of spectacular valleys and peaks over 3000 metres. What's it called?

A Alps   B Carpathians   C Pyrenees

3. Until 1990 Germany was divided into two nations and had two capital cities. One of them became the present-day capital of reunified Germany. Do you know its name?

A Berlin   B Hamburg   C Frankfurt

...FUN FACT...

Paris is home to the most visited art museum in the world. Over 8 million people enter the Louvre every year to admire some of the most important art works of every era. The museum is so big that altogether the rooms take up the same area as approximately 9 football pitches!

"All roads lead to Rome". This proverb refers to the incredible network of roads built by the Ancient Romans during the expansion of their empire towards the European borders. Considerably reducing the travel times of armies and goods, it was actually the roads that allowed the Romans to dominate all the countries around the Mediterranean for many centuries. Tarmac has now replaced the stones, but Europe's greatest connecting roads are still the same.

13

SWITZERLAND
Capital: Bern
Population: 7 593 494

14

LIECHTENSTEIN
Capital: Vaduz
Population: 35 446

15

AUSTRIA
Capital: Vienna
Population: 8 342 600

16

SAN MARINO
Capital: San Marino
Population: 19 149

17

SLOVENIA
Capital: Ljubljana
Population: 2 025 866

18

CROATIA
Capital: Zagreb
Population: 4 432 000

19

BOSNIA AND HERZEGOVINA
Capital: Sarajevo
Population: 3 940 400

20

VATICAN CITY
Capital: Vatican City
Population: 506

21

ITALY
Capital: Rome
Population: 60 045 068

22

MALTA
Capital: Valletta
Population: 404 962

...DID YOU KNOW THAT...

Scandinavia and Russia occupy the taiga (also known as the boreal forest), a non-stop band of woods and forests that cover all of the surfaces around the Arctic Circle (therefore also Canada and America).
The taiga is a precious environment for mankind as the billions of trees there are the greatest forest reserve on our planet.

EUROPEAN COUNTRIES

23

ICELAND
Capital: Reykjavík
Population: 319 756

24

NORWAY
Capital: Oslo
Population: 4 799 252

25

SWEDEN
Capital: Stockholm
Population: 9 256 347

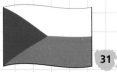
26

FINLAND
Capital: Helsinki
Population: 5 326 314

27

RUSSIA
Capital: Moscow
Population: 141 780 000

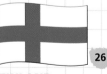
28

ESTONIA
Capital: Tallinn
Population: 10 340 935

29

LATVIA
Capital: Rīga
Population: 2 270 894

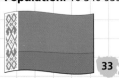
30

LITHUANIA
Capital: Vilnius
Population: 3 350 079

31

CZECH REPUBLIC
Capital: Prague
Population: 10 381 130

32

POLAND
Capital: Warsaw
Population: 38 135 876

33

BELARUS
Capital: Minsk
Population: 9 690 000

34

SLOVAKIA
Capital: Bratislava
Population: 5 412 254

GEO...QUIZ!

1. The most northerly point of Norway is also the most northerly point in Europe. What's the name of this distant place?

A Cabo de Fisterre   B North Cape   C Cape Horn

2. The Czech Republic is a young nation, created in 1993 by the peaceful separation from Slovakia. What is its capital?

A Prague   B Bratislava   C Budapest

3. The Danube flows through most of Europe and 4 capital cities rise along its 2888 kilometres. Which sea does it flow into?

A Mediterranean   B Adriatic   C Black

4. Europe is home to the world's youngest country, only independent since 2006. The capital is Podgorica and the country is...

A Croatia   B Montenegro   C Estonia

...FUN FACT...

St. Basil's Cathedral marks the geometric centre of Moscow, the capital of Russia. Its multicoloured architecture and spires aim to represent the fire of the faithful that rises up into the sky. The cathedral is formed by nine churches, each of which is devoted to a different saint. Built in the sixteenth century, it dominates Red Square and the Kremlin, symbols of Russian political power.

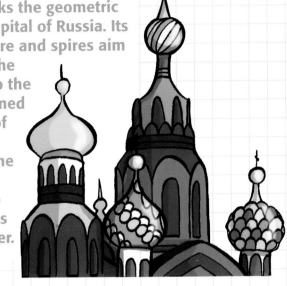

The capital of Greece, Athens is a metropolis of over 3 million inhabitants. At the centre of the city, perched on a rock that's about 100 metres high, isolated from the city's traffic, stands the Acropolis, centre of the usually fortified, ancient Greek cities, which was home to the main religious and political buildings. The one in Athens is undoubtedly the most famous and striking. Here you find the Parthenon, the temple dedicated to the goddess Athena. On the Acropolis you can visit other monuments and the most important archaeological museum in Greece.

 35

UKRAINE
Capital: Kiev
Population: 46 044 718

 36

HUNGARY
Capital: Budapest
Population: 10 045 401

37

ROMANIA
Capital: Bucharest
Population: 21 508 000

38

MOLDOVA
Capital: Kishinev
Population: 3 958 000

 39

MONTENEGRO
Capital: Podgorica
Population: 627 000

 40

SERBIA
Capital: Belgrade
Population: 9 880 000

41

BULGARIA
Capital: Sofia
Population: 7 640 238

 42

ALBANIA
Capital: Tirana
Population: 3 174 000

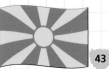 43

MACEDONIA
Capital: Skopje
Population: 2 045 177

 44

GREECE
Capital: Athens
Population: 11 215 785

ASIA, PHYSICAL

32

0 400 800 1200 1600 2000 km
Scale 1 : 42 000 000

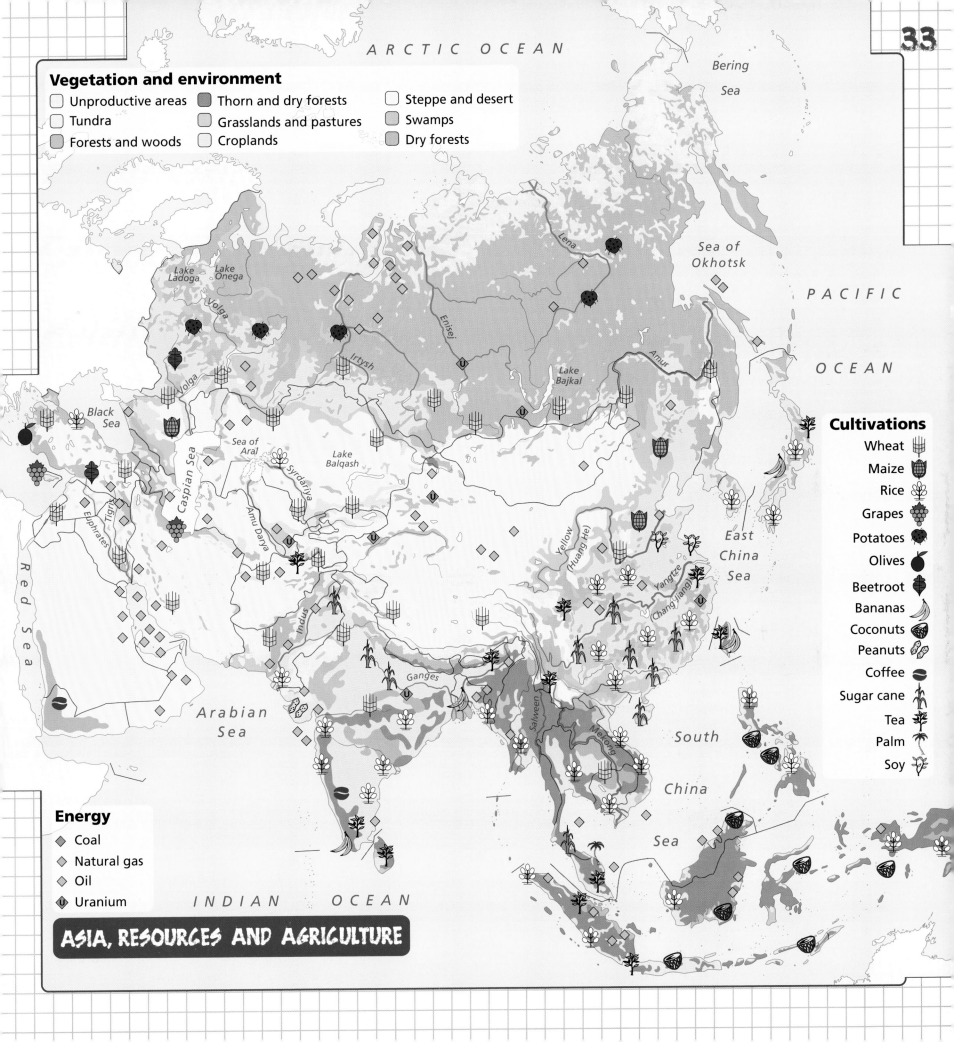

Vegetation and environment

- ☐ Unproductive areas
- ☐ Tundra
- ☐ Forests and woods
- ☐ Thorn and dry forests
- ☐ Grasslands and pastures
- ☐ Croplands
- ☐ Steppe and desert
- ☐ Swamps
- ☐ Dry forests

Cultivations

- Wheat
- Maize
- Rice
- Grapes
- Potatoes
- Olives
- Beetroot
- Bananas
- Coconuts
- Peanuts
- Coffee
- Sugar cane
- Tea
- Palm
- Soy

Energy

- ◆ Coal
- ◆ Natural gas
- ◆ Oil
- ⓤ Uranium

ASIA, RESOURCES AND AGRICULTURE

ARCTIC OCEAN

Bering Sea

PACIFIC OCEAN

Sea of Okhotsk

Lake Ladoga
Lake Onega
Volga
Lena
Enisei
Irtysh
Amur
Lake Bajkal
Black Sea
Sea of Aral
Lake Balqash
Caspian Sea
Syrdarja
Amu Darja
Red Sea
Tigris
Euphrates
Indus
Ganges
Yellow (Huang He)
Yangtze (Chang Jiang)
Salween
Mekong
East China Sea
South China Sea
Arabian Sea
INDIAN OCEAN

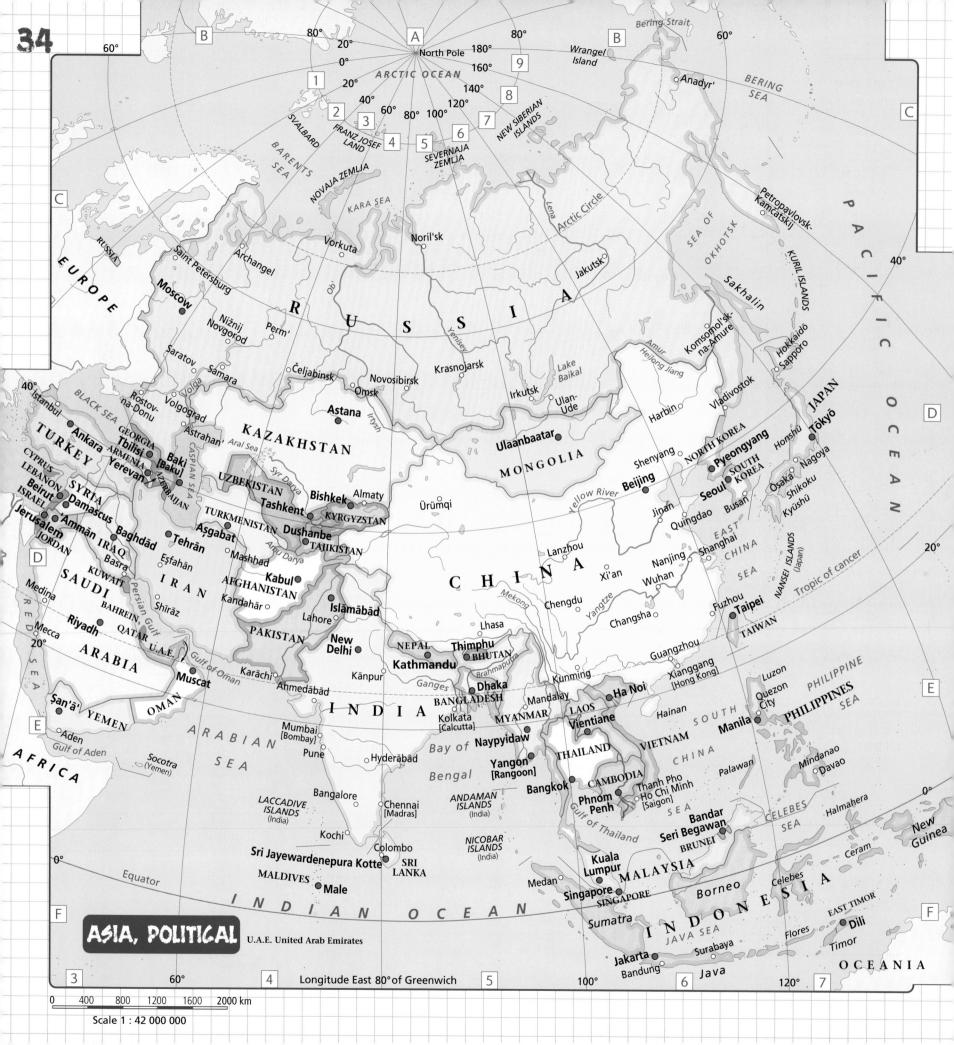

34

ASIA, POLITICAL

U.A.E. United Arab Emirates

Longitude East 80° of Greenwich

0 400 800 1200 1600 2000 km

Scale 1 : 42 000 000

ARCTIC OCEAN

Bering Sea

Most populated areas
(number of inhabitants per km²)

- more than 500
- 100 - 200
- 50 - 100
- 25 - 50
- 10 - 25
- 1 - 10
- 0 - 1
- uninhabited areas

Sea of Okhotsk

Moscow

Ekaterinburg

Čeljabinsk

Omsk • Novosibirsk

Sapporo

Harbin

İstanbul

Black Sea

İzmir • Ankara

Tbilisi

Ulaanbaatar

Shenyang
Pyeongyang

Tōkyō

Yokohama

Yerevan

Beijing

Seoul

Beirut
el Aviv-Yafo • Aleppo

Baki

Almaty

Busan

Ōsaka

Damascus

Caspian Sea

Taiyuan

Tianjin

Ammān
Baghdād

Tehrān

Tashkent

Nanjing

East China Sea

Esfāhān

Kabul

Rawalpindi

Chengdu

Wuhan

Shanghai

Riyadh

Shīrāz

Lahore

Kathmandu

Chongqing

Taipei

PACIFIC OCEAN

Jiddah

Kārachi

Delhi

Guangzhou

Kānpur

Dhāka

Şan'ā'

Ahmedābād

Kolkata
[Calcutta]

Chittagong

Hanoi

Quezon City

Urban inhabitants

- 1 000 000 - 2 500 000
- 2 500 000 - 5 000 000
- 5 000 000 - 10 000 000
- more than 10 000 000

Nāgpur

Mumbai
[Bombay]

Pune
Hyderābād

Yangon
[Rangoon]

South China Sea

Manila

Davao

Krung Thep

Bangalore • Chennai
[Madras]

Phnom
Penh

Thanh Pho
Ho Chi Minh
[Saigon]

Colombo

ASIA, POPULATION

INDIAN OCEAN

Medan

Kuala Laumpur

Makassar

Jakarta

Surabaya

Bandung

...DID YOU KNOW THAT...

Due to the sale of oil, the Arab nations around the Persian Gulf have made a lot of money and, particularly in Dubai in the United Arab Emirates, real metropolises are being built along the desert coasts with extremely tall skyscrapers, man-made islands shaped like palms, shopping centres frequented by consumers from all over the world and even a 400-metre-long ski slope in an enormous hanger in the middle of the desert.

ASIAN COUNTRIES

TURKEY
Capital: Ankara
Population: 71 517 000

GEORGIA
Capital: Tbilisi
Population: 4 659 100

KAZAKHSTAN
Capital: Astana
Population: 15 571 506

CYPRUS
Capital: Nicosia
Population: 789 300

ARMENIA
Capital: Yerevan
Population: 3 230 000

AZERBAIJAN
Capital: Baki [Baku]
Population: 8 629 900

UZBEKISTAN
Capital: Tashkent
Population: 27 313 700

KYRGYZSTAN
Capital: Bishkek
Population: 5 262 300

LEBANON
Capital: Beirut
Population: 4 140 000

SYRIA
Capital: Damascus
Population: 19 880 000

TURKMENISTAN
Capital: Ashgabat
Population: 5 900 000

TAJIKISTAN
Capital: Dushanbe
Population: 7 215 000

ISRAEL
Capital: Jerusalem
Population: 7 202 000

JORDAN
Capital: Amman
Population: 5 906 000

GEO...QUIZ!

1. The world's biggest lake is found in Asia. It's so big that it's called a sea. What's its name?

A Aral   B Caspian   C Baikal

2. Mesopotamia is often referred to as "the cradle of the great civilisations": the Sumerians, Babylonians, Assyrians, etc. In which country is it now found?

A Iraq   B Iran   C Jordan

3. Kabul is the capital of a country sadly known for the ongoing wars that have stained it with blood for many years. Which country are we talking about?

A Oman   B Yemen   C Afghanistan

4. There's only one big island in the Mediterranean that is regarded as Asian. It is partly occupied by Turkey. Which is it?

A Socotra   B Cyprus   C Sakhalin

...FUN FACT...

Siberia occupies the whole of the northern part of Asia and until 1903 a journey through these lands took 4 months even in the summer.
What happened in 1903?
After 12 years of work, the world's longest railway was opened: the Trans-Siberian.
Setting off from Moscow, the city of Vladivostok on the Sea of Japan could be reached in a week. The figures of this incredible feat of human engineering are impressive: 9288 kilometres long, more than 100 stops and passing through 7 time zones. Up to 90 000 people worked at any one time to build it, many of whom were prisoners sentenced to hard labour.

IRAQ
Capital: Baghdad
Population: 28 500 000

IRAN
Capital: Tehran
Population: 72 213 000

AFGHANISTAN
Capital: Kabul
Population: 30 190 000

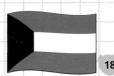

KUWAIT
Capital: Kuwait City
Population: 2 640 000

SAUDI ARABIA
Capital: Riyadh
Population: 24 810 000

BAHRAIN
Capital: Manama
Population: 1 046 000

QATAR
Capital: Doha
Population: 791 000

UNITED ARAB EMIRATES
Capital: Abu Dhabi
Population: 4 765 000

YEMEN
Capital: Sanaa
Population: 22 198 000

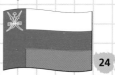

OMAN
Capital: Muscat
Population: 2 909 000

...DID YOU KNOW THAT...

One of the world's biggest deserts lies between Mongolia and China. It's the Gobi, which actually means "desert" in the Mongol language. Its extreme characteristics (40° C in the summer, -40° C in the winter and big sandstorms in the spring) make it a hard area to explore. However, it's a sort of paradise for palaeontologists (the academics who look for fossils). Since 1922 hundreds of dinosaur

fossils have been found, which, due to the conservation conditions beneath the compacted desert sand, are often virtually intact.

Carcharodontosaurus

EUROPEAN RUSSIA

ASIATIC RUSSIA

ASIAN COUNTRIES

MONGOLIA
Capital: Ulaanbaatar
Population: 2 682 416
25

NORTH KOREA
Capital: Pyongyang
Population: 24 051 218
26

SOUTH KOREA
Capital: Seoul
Population: 48 600 000
27

JAPAN
Capital: Tokyo
Population: 127 931 339
28

PAKISTAN
Capital: Islamabad
Population: 163 077 500
29

NEPAL
Capital: Kathmandu
Population: 26 966 600
30

BHUTAN
Capital: Thimphu
Population: 671 000
31

CHINA
Capital: Beijing
Population: 1 321 290 000
32

TAIWAN
Capital: Taipei
Population: 22 958 000
33

INDIA
Capital: New Delhi
Population: 1 147 677 000
34

BANGLADESH
Capital: Dhaka
Population: 146 020 000
35

MYANMAR
Capital: Yangon, Naypyidaw
Population: 49 221 000
36

LAOS
Capital: Vientiane
Population: 5 965 000
37

THAILAND
Capital: Bangkok
Population: 66 150 000
38

GEO...QUIZ!

1. With over 1 billion and 300 million inhabitants, this nation is the most populous in the world. Which country are we talking about?

A India   B China   C Indonesia

Japan is called the Land of the Rising Sun as it's situated in the East, right where the Sun rises. What's its capital?

A Tōkyō   B Beijing   C Seoul

3. The island of Ceylon rises up to the south of India, famous for its tea plantations. With its independence from the United Kingdom, the country regained its original name, which is?

A Celebes   B Bali   C Sri Lanka

4. At the southernmost end of the Malay Peninsula, there's an independent, rich and modern city-state. What's it called?

A Hong Kong   B Singapore   C Macau

...FUN FACT...

The tiger is, without a doubt, the animal that symbolises Asia. Its name comes from the Persian "tigris", which means arrow and refers to the speed of the feline. There are many tiger sub-species; some – like the Siberian tiger – have a stripe-less coat as they live in different environments than the tropical forest where the stripes help them to camouflage with the shade of the trees during hunting. Through deforestation, the tiger has now lost 93% of its habitat and the species is at risk of extinction due to hunting and the use of its body parts in traditional Asian medicine.

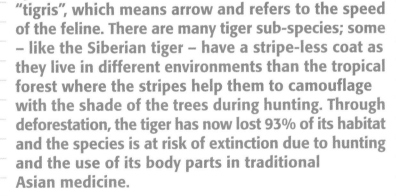

 39

CAMBODIA
Capital: Phnom Penh
Population: 13 388 000

 40

VIETNAM
Capital: Hanoi
Population: 86 211 000

 41

PHILIPPINES
Capital: Manila
Population: 90 346 000

 42

MALDIVES
Capital: Male
Population: 309 575

 43

SRI LANKA
Capital: Sri Jayewaderenepura Kotte
Population: 20 135 000

 44

MALAYSIA
Capital: Kuala Lumpur
Population: 27 730 000

 45

BRUNEI
Capital: Bandar Seri Begawan
Population: 396 000

 46

SINGAPORE
Capital: Singapore
Population: 3 642 700

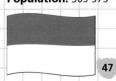 47

INDONESIA
Capital: Jakarta
Population: 228 523 300

 48

TIMOR-LESTE
Capital: Dili
Population: 1 125 000

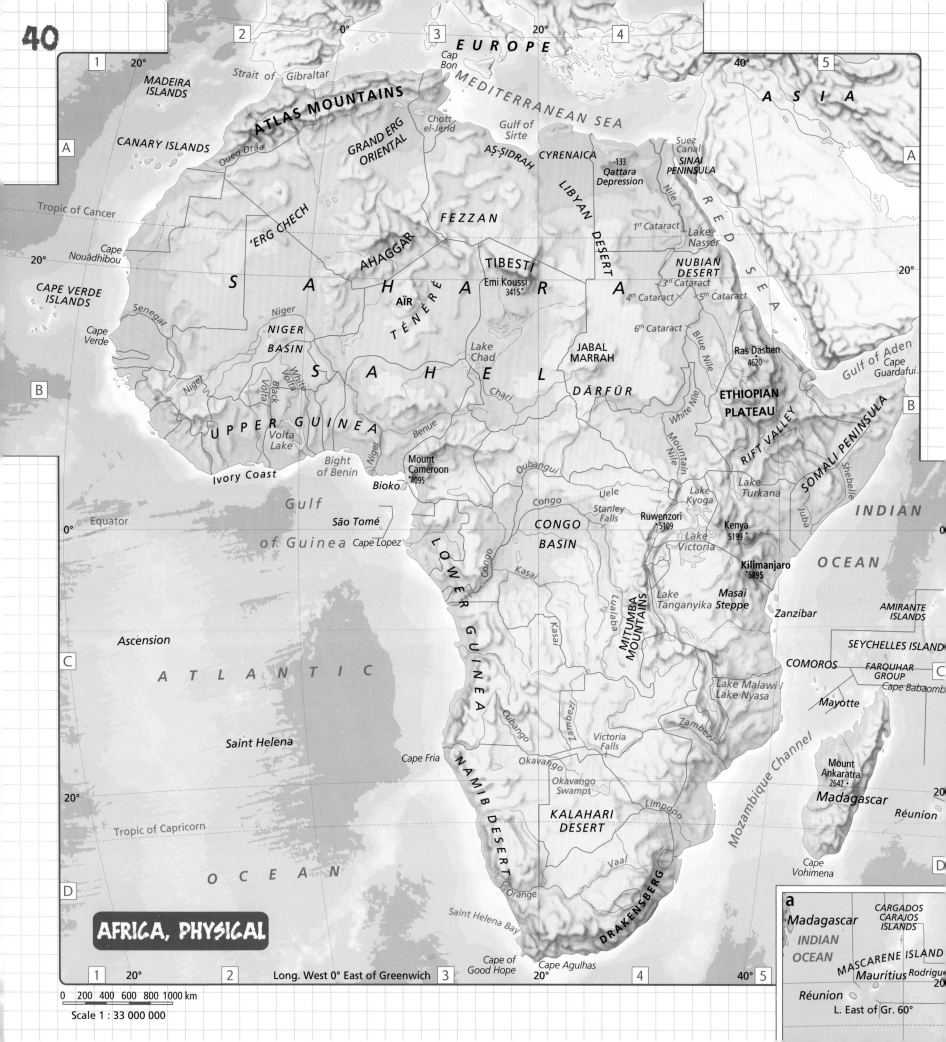

40

EUROPE

ASIA

MADEIRA ISLANDS

Strait of Gibraltar

Cap Bon

MEDITERRANEAN SEA

CANARY ISLANDS

ATLAS MOUNTAINS

GRAND ERG ORIENTAL

Chott el-Jerid

Gulf of Sirte

AṢ-ṢIDRAH

CYRENAICA

-133 Qattara Depression

Suez Canal

SINAI PENINSULA

Oued Drâa

Tropic of Cancer

Cape Nouâdhibou

'ERG CHECH

LIBYAN DESERT

1st Cataract

Lake Nasser

Nile

CAPE VERDE ISLANDS

Cape Verde

20°

S   A

AHAGGAR

FEZZAN

TIBESTI

Emi Koussi 3415

H   A   R   A

NUBIAN DESERT

3rd Cataract

4th Cataract   5th Cataract

RED SEA

Senegal

Niger

AÏR

TÉNÉRÉ

6th Cataract

JABAL MARRAH

Ras Dashen 4620

Gulf of Aden

Cape Guardafui

NIGER BASIN

Niger

Lake Chad

White Volta

Black Volta

S   A   H   E   L

DĀRFŪR

ETHIOPIAN PLATEAU

Chari

White Nile

Blue Nile

SOMALI PENINSULA

UPPER GUINEA

Volta Lake

Benue

Niger

RIFT VALLEY

Shebelle

Ivory Coast

Bight of Benin

Mount Cameroon 4095

Mountain Nile

Lake Turkana

Juba

Bioko

Gulf

Oubangui

Uele

Lake Kyoga

INDIAN

São Tomé

of Guinea

Cape Lopez

Congo

CONGO BASIN

Stanley Falls

Ruwenzori 5109

Kenya 5199

Equator

LOWER

Congo

Kasai

Lake Victoria

OCEAN

GUINEA

Kasai

Lualaba

Kilimanjaro 5895

Masai Steppe

Zanzibar

AMIRANTE ISLANDS

Ascension

ATLANTIC

Lake Tanganyika

MITUMBA MOUNTAINS

SEYCHELLES ISLAND

COMOROS

FARQUHAR GROUP

Cape Babaomb

Saint Helena

Lake Malawi / Lake Nyasa

Mayotte

Cubango

Zambezi

NAMIB

Cape Fria

Okavango

Victoria Falls

Zambezi

Mozambique Channel

Mount Ankaratra 2642

Madagascar

Réunion

OCEAN

Okavango Swamps

DESERT

KALAHARI DESERT

Limpopo

Tropic of Capricorn

Vaal

Cape Vohimena

Saint Helena Bay

DRAKENSBERG

Orange

AFRICA, PHYSICAL

Cape of Good Hope

Cape Agulhas

Long. West 0° East of Greenwich

20°

40°

a

Madagascar

INDIAN OCEAN

CARGADOS CARAJOS ISLANDS

MASCARENE ISLAND

Mauritius

Rodrigu

Réunion

L. East of Gr. 60°

0   200   400   600   800 1000 km

Scale 1 : 33 000 000

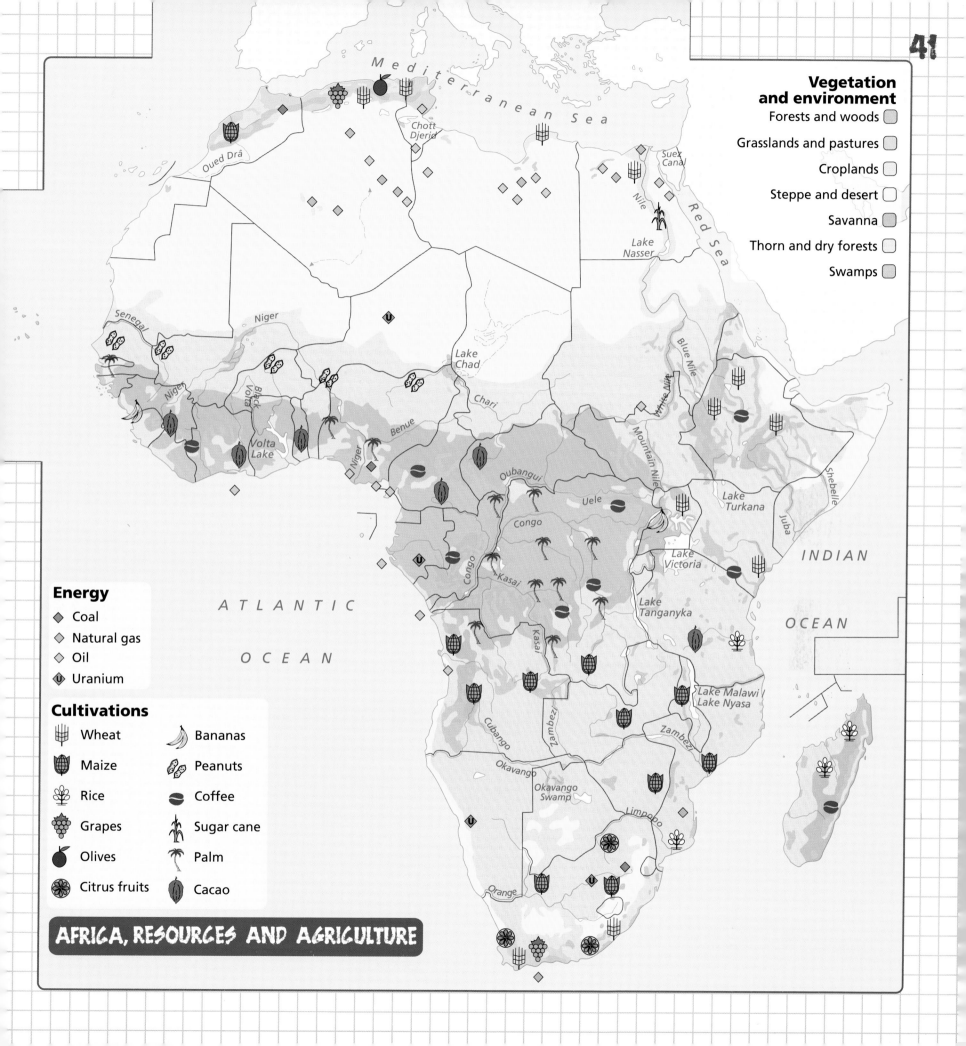

Vegetation and environment

Forests and woods
Grasslands and pastures
Croplands
Steppe and desert
Savanna
Thorn and dry forests
Swamps

Energy

◆ Coal
◇ Natural gas
◇ Oil
Ⓤ Uranium

Cultivations

Wheat   Bananas
Maize   Peanuts
Rice   Coffee
Grapes   Sugar cane
Olives   Palm
Citrus fruits   Cacao

AFRICA, RESOURCES AND AGRICULTURE

Mediterranean Sea
Chott Djerid
Oued Drâ
Senegal
Niger
Black Volta
Volta Lake
Niger
Benue
Lake Chad
Chari
Oubangui
Congo
Uele
Kasai
Congo
Kasai
Cubango
Zambezi
Okavango
Okavango Swamp
Zambezi
Limpopo
Orange
Lake Nasser
Nile
Red Sea
Suez Canal
Blue Nile
White Nile
Mountain Nile
Lake Turkana
Shebelle
Juba
Lake Victoria
Lake Tanganyka
Lake Malawi / Lake Nyasa
INDIAN OCEAN
ATLANTIC OCEAN

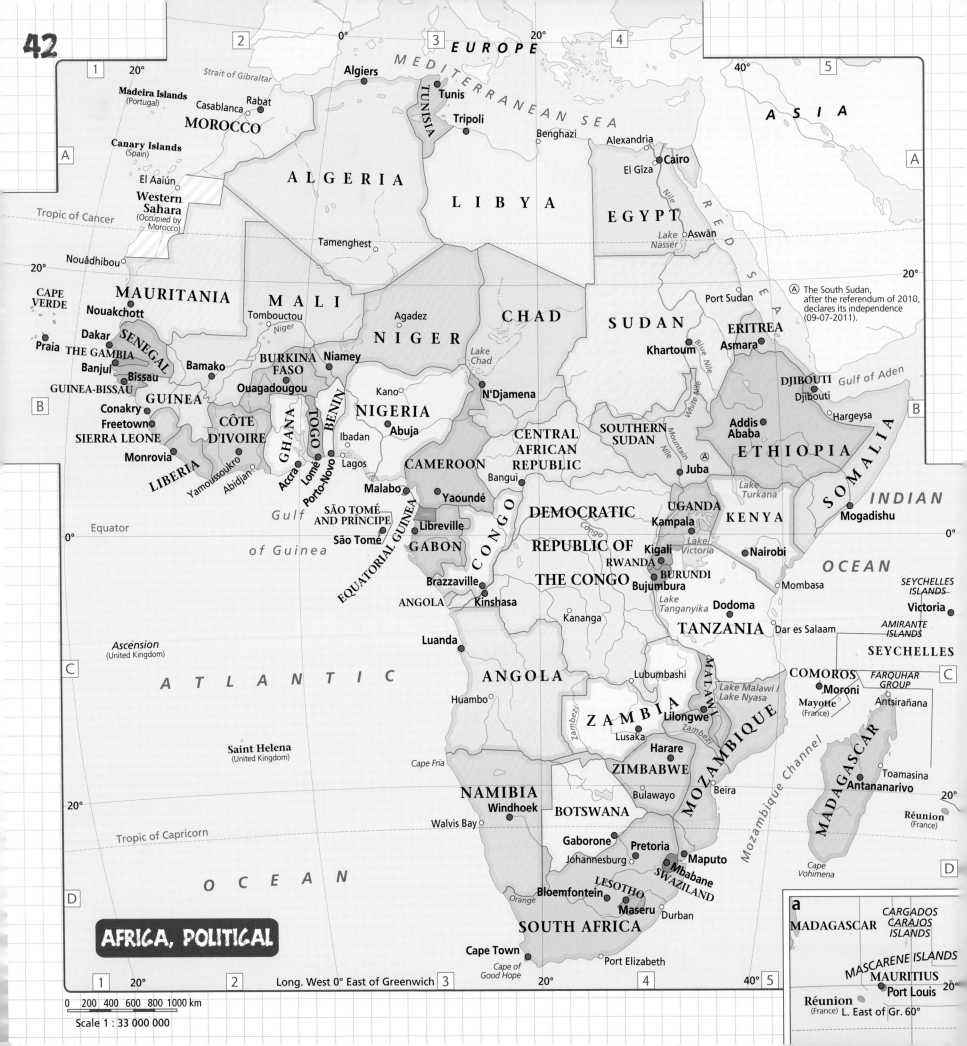

1 20°   2   0°   3   *EUROPE* 20°   4   40°   5

MEDITERRANEAN SEA

Strait of Gibraltar

Madeira Islands
(Portugal)

Algiers

Tunis
TUNISIA
Tripoli

Benghazi

Alexandria
El Gîza Cairo

ASIA

Casablanca Rabat

A Canary Islands
(Spain)

MOROCCO

ALGERIA

LIBYA

EGYPT

El Aaiún

Tropic of Cancer

**Western
Sahara**
(Occupied by
Morocco)

Nile

Lake
Nasser

Aswân

(A) The South Sudan,
after the referendum of 2010,
declares its independence
(09-07-2011).

20° Nouâdhibou

Tamenghest

20°

Port Sudan

CAPE
VERDE

MAURITANIA

MALI

Agadez

CHAD

SUDAN

RED SEA

ERITREA

Nouakchott

Tombouctou

Niger

NIGER

Lake
Chad

Khartoum

Asmara

Blue Nile

Dakar
Praia   SENEGAL
THE GAMBIA
Banjul   Bamako
Bissau
GUINEA-BISSAU   GUINEA
Conakry   CÔTE
Freetown   D'IVOIRE
SIERRA LEONE
Monrovia   LIBERIA
Yamoussoukro
Abidjan

**BURKINA
FASO**   Niamey
Ouagadougou

GHANA TOGO BENIN

Kano

NIGERIA
Ibadan Abuja
Accra Lomé Lagos
Porto-Novo
Malabo

N'Djamena

**CENTRAL
AFRICAN
REPUBLIC**

**SOUTHERN
SUDAN**

White Nile

Mountain Nile

Juba

DJIBOUTI
Djibouti

Hargeysa

Addis
Ababa

ETHIOPIA

B

B

Gulf of Aden

SOMALIA

CAMEROON

Bangui

Yaoundé

SÃO TOMÉ
AND PRÍNCIPE

São Tomé

Gulf
of Guinea

EQUATORIAL GUINEA

Libreville

GABON

Brazzaville

ANGOLA Kinshasa

DEMOCRATIC

REPUBLIC OF

CONGO

Congo

THE CONGO

Kananga

UGANDA
Kampala

Kigali
RWANDA
BURUNDI
Bujumbura

Lake
Victoria

KENYA

Lake
Turkana

Nairobi

Mogadishu

INDIAN

OCEAN

SEYCHELLES
ISLANDS

Victoria

Equator 0°

0°

Mombasa

AMIRANTE
ISLANDS

SEYCHELLES

Ascension
(United Kingdom)

A T L A N T I C

ANGOLA

Lake
Tanganyika

Dodoma

TANZANIA

Dar es Salaam

COMOROS
Moroni

FARQUHAR
GROUP

C

C

Luanda

Lubumbashi

Lake Malawi /
Lake Nyasa

Mayotte
(France)

Antsirañana

Huambo

Zambezi

ZAMBIA

MALAWI
Lilongwe

Mozambique Channel

Saint Helena
(United Kingdom)

Lusaka

Harare

Zambezi

MADAGASCAR

Cape Fria

ZIMBABWE

MOZAMBIQUE

Toamasina

Antananarivo

Bulawayo

Beira

20°

NAMIBIA   Windhoek

BOTSWANA

Réunion
(France)

20°

Walvis Bay

Tropic of Capricorn

Gaborone

Pretoria

Cape
Vohimena

D

Johannesburg
Orange

Maputo
Mbabane
SWAZILAND

O C E A N

Bloemfontein   LESOTHO
Maseru   Durban

SOUTH AFRICA

a
MADAGASCAR

CARGADOS
CARAJOS
ISLANDS

AFRICA, POLITICAL

Cape Town
Cape of
Good Hope

Port Elizabeth

MASCARENE ISLANDS

MAURITIUS

Port Louis

Réunion
(France) L. East of Gr. 60°

0   200 400 600 800 1000 km

Scale 1 : 33 000 000

1 20°   2   Long. West 0° East of Greenwich 3   20°   4   40° 5

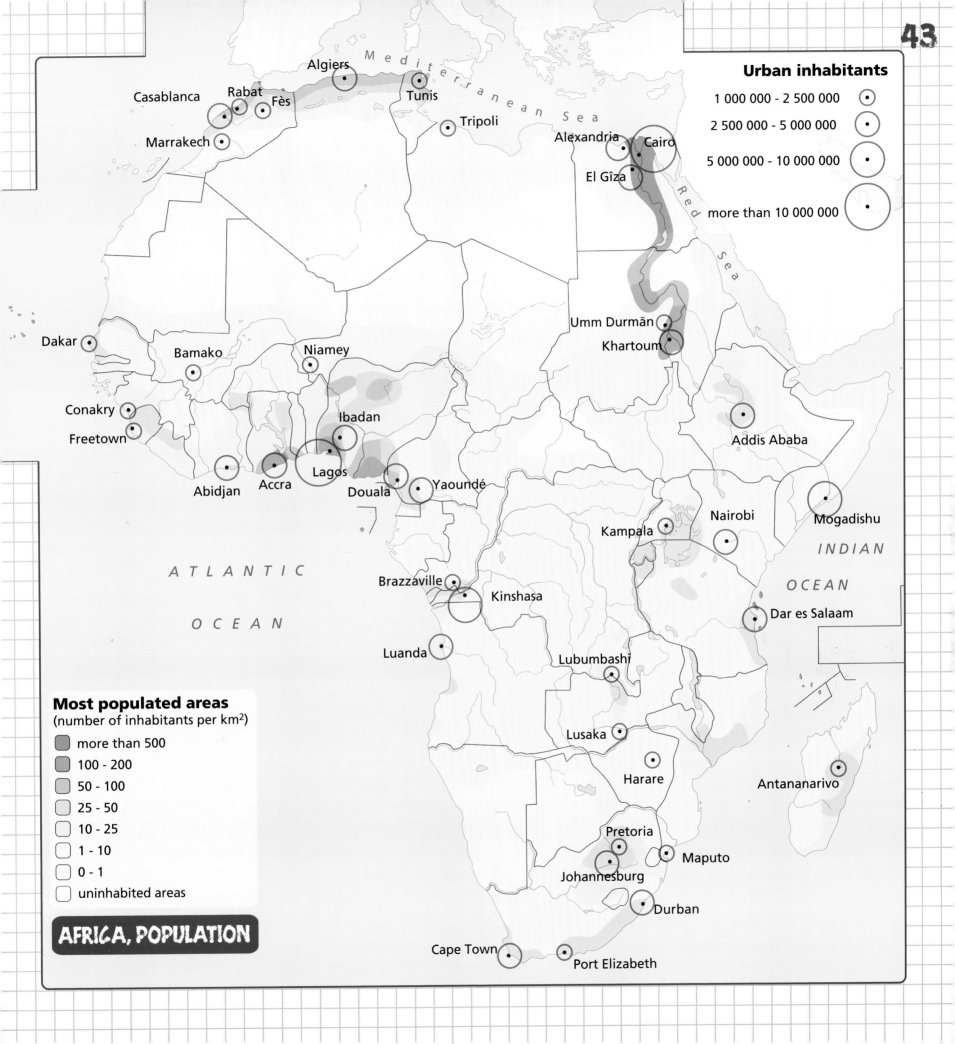

Urban inhabitants

1 000 000 - 2 500 000

2 500 000 - 5 000 000

5 000 000 - 10 000 000

more than 10 000 000

Mediterranean Sea

Casablanca Rabat
Algiers
Fès Tunis
Marrakech Tripoli
Alexandria Cairo
El Gîza
Red Sea

Dakar
Bamako
Niamey
Umm Durmān
Khartoum

Conakry
Freetown
Ibadan
Addis Ababa

Abidjan Accra Lagos
Douala Yaoundé

A T L A N T I C

Kampala Nairobi Mogadishu

I N D I A N

O C E A N

Brazzaville
Kinshasa

O C E A N

Dar es Salaam

Luanda
Lubumbashi

Lusaka

Harare

Antananarivo

Most populated areas
(number of inhabitants per km²)

more than 500

100 - 200

50 - 100

25 - 50

10 - 25

1 - 10

0 - 1

uninhabited areas

Pretoria
Maputo

Johannesburg

Durban

AFRICA, POPULATION

Cape Town
Port Elizabeth

...DID YOU KNOW THAT...

On the Giza Plateau, in Egypt, the Great Pyramid of Cheops rises 146 metres, the Pyramid of Khafre reaches 144 metres and Menkaure 65 metres.
The four sides of the Great Pyramid are perfectly aligned with the four compass points and it was covered with white marble in antiquity. It was the world's highest building for almost 4000 years until 1311, when it was surpassed by Lincoln Cathedral in England.

Western Sahara (occupied by Morocco)

AFRICAN COUNTRIES

MOROCCO
Capital: Rabat
Population: 31 130 000

ALGERIA
Capital: Algiers
Population: 34 460 000

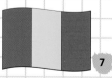

TUNISIA
Capital: Tunis
Population: 10 327 000

LIBYA
Capital: Tripoli
Population: 6 000 000

EGYPT
Capital: Cairo
Population: 75 700 000

MAURITANIA
Capital: Nouakchott
Population: 3 161 000

MALI
Capital: Bamako
Population: 12 716 000

NIGER
Capital: Niamey
Population: 14 296 816

CHAD
Capital: N'Djamena
Population: 10 435 000

SUDAN
Capital: Khartoum
Population: 39 154 000

ERITREA
Capital: Asmara
Population: 4 675 000

CAPE VERDE
Capital: Praia
Population: 508 000

SENEGAL
Capital: Dakar
Population: 11 660 000

THE GAMBIA
Capital: Banjul
Population: 1 594 000

GEO...QUIZ!

1. Dakar was the destination of an international car rally for many years. Of which country is it the capital?

A Guinea   B Mauritania   C Senegal

2. Sudan is crossed by the longest river in Africa. Which is it?

A Congo   B Niger   C Nile

3. Algeria's economy is based on the extraction of oil, but fishing is also important. Which sea do the Algerian ports overlook?

A Red   B Mediterranean   C Black

4. Morocco is famous for certain cities that were home to the various royal dynasties over the centuries. One of these became the capital. Which is it?

A Fès   B Marrakech   C Rabat

...FUN FACT...

300 000 years ago, the Sahara Desert was a dense forest populated by many animals and ancient populations that depended on animal husbandry and hunting. The numerous rock engravings bear witness to this.

The Tuareg are nomadic people in the Sahara Desert and are known as the Blue People due to their custom of covering their faces with a blue veil. Descendants of the ancient Berber tribe, they learned to find their way around the monotonous desert dunes with the Sun and the stars. They move around on camels and were recently recognised by the UN as "indigenous people", meaning that they have a close bond with their land.

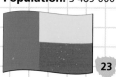 **15**

GUINEA-BISSAU
Capital: Bissau
Population: 1 424 000

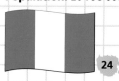 **16**

GUINEA
Capital: Conakry
Population: 8 515 000

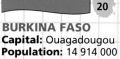 **17**

SIERRA LEONE
Capital: Freetown
Population: 5 550 000

 **18**

LIBERIA
Capital: Monrovia
Population: 3 489 000

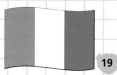 **19**

CÔTE D'IVORE
Capital: Yamoussoukro
Population: 20 798 000

 **20**

BURKINA FASO
Capital: Ouagadougou
Population: 14 914 000

 **21**

GHANA
Capital: Accra
Population: 22 470 000

 **22**

TOGO
Capital: Lomé
Population: 5 615 000

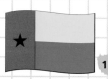 **23**

BENIN
Capital: Porto-Novo
Population: 8 267 000

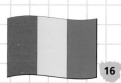 **24**

NIGERIA
Capital: Abuja
Population: 146 390 000

 **25**

ETHIOPIA
Capital: Addis Ababa
Population: 75 690 000

 **26**

DJIBOUTI
Capital: Djibouti
Population: 730 000

 **27**

SOMALIA
Capital: Mogadishu
Population: 9 400 000

...DID YOU KNOW THAT...

The mountain gorilla lives in the forests on the border between Uganda and the Democratic Republic of the Congo.
It is the biggest species of apes currently in existence on the planet. Just think that an adult male can weigh 200 kilos and eat up to 34 kilos of leaves, shoots and bark! Due to hunting and the civil war in the Congo, mountain gorillas are on the brink of extinction.

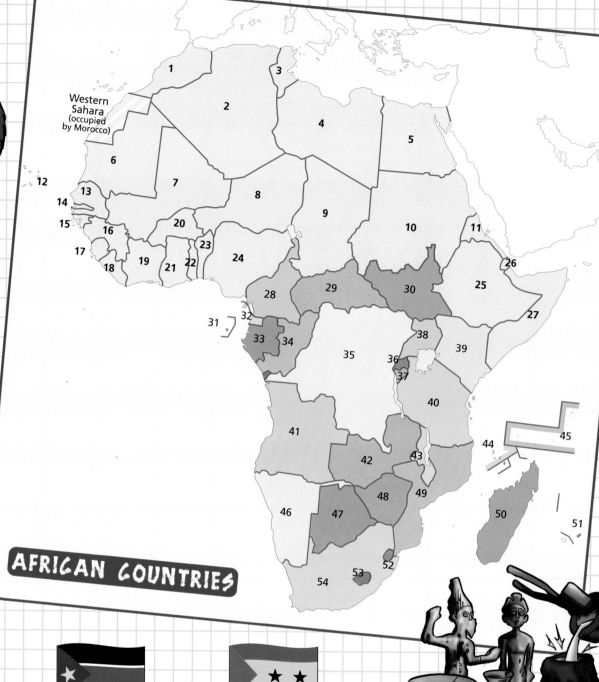

Western Sahara (occupied by Morocco)

AFRICAN COUNTRIES

28

CAMEROON
Capital: Yaoundé
Population: 18 165 000

29

CENTRAL AFRICAN REPUBLIC
Capital: Bangui
Population: 4 226 000

30

SOUTHERN SUDAN
Capital: Juba
Population: 143 000

31

SÃO TOMÉ AND PRÍNCIPE
Capital: São Tomé
Population: 158 000

32

EQUATORIAL GUINEA
Capital: Malabo
Population: 1 180 000

33

GABON
Capital: Libreville
Population: 1 375 000

34

CONGO
Capital: Brazzaville
Population: 3 734 000

35

DEM. REPUBLIC OF THE CONGO
Capital: Kinshasa
Population: 64 704 000

36

RWANDA
Capital: Kigali
Population: 9 330 000

37

BURUNDI
Capital: Bujumbura
Population: 7 903 000

38

UGANDA
Capital: Kampala
Population: 29 230 000

39

KENYA
Capital: Nairobi
Population: 35 112 000

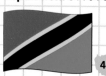
40

TANZANIA
Capital: Dodoma
Population: 40 800 000

41

ANGOLA
Capital: Luanda
Population: 16 850 000

GEO...QUIZ!

1. In the middle of the continent there are two nations whose names include the word "Congo". But what is the Congo?

A a mount   **B** a lake   **C** a river

2. Namibia is home to the world's most famous coastal desert: the Namib. Onto which ocean do its two highest sand dunes face?

A Pacific   **B** Atlantic   **C** Indian

3. The largest African island is home to a type of animals that are only found there: lemurs, also known as prosimians. Do you know which country we're talking about?

A Madagascar   **B** Zanzibar   **C** Réunion

4. Kenya gained independence from the English in 1963 and it is now one of the greatest tourist destinations in Africa. What's its capital?

A Dodoma   **B** Kampala   **C** Nairobi

...FUN FACT...

South Africa is the southernmost country on the continent and is home to all the natural environments that can be encountered in Africa. The south coast enjoys a climate similar to the Mediterranean, whereas there's the desert to the west. The grassy plains of the savannah extend to the north, home to the most famous of African animals like the lion, elephant and giraffe. Lastly, strips of tropical forest are found along the rivers.

 42

ZAMBIA
Capital: Lusaka
Population: 11 880 000

 43

MALAWI
Capital: Lilongwe
Population: 13 066 000

 44

COMOROS
Capital: Moroni
Population: 646 000

 45

SEYCHELLES
Capital: Victoria
Population: 87 000

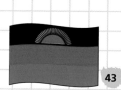 46

NAMIBIA
Capital: Windhoek
Population: 2 054 000

 47

BOTSWANA
Capital: Gaborone
Population: 1 816 000

 48

ZIMBABWE
Capital: Harare
Population: 12 170 000

49

MOZAMBIQUE
Capital: Maputo
Population: 21 020 000

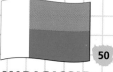 50

MADAGASCAR
Capital: Antananarivo
Population: 18 866 000

 51

MAURITIUS
Capital: Port Louis
Population: 1 269 000

 52

LESOTHO
Capital: Maseru
Population: 1 910 000

 53

SWAZILAND
Capital: Mbabane
Population: 963 000

54

SOUTH AFRICA
Capital: Cape Town, Bloemfontein, Pretoria
Population: 49 320 000

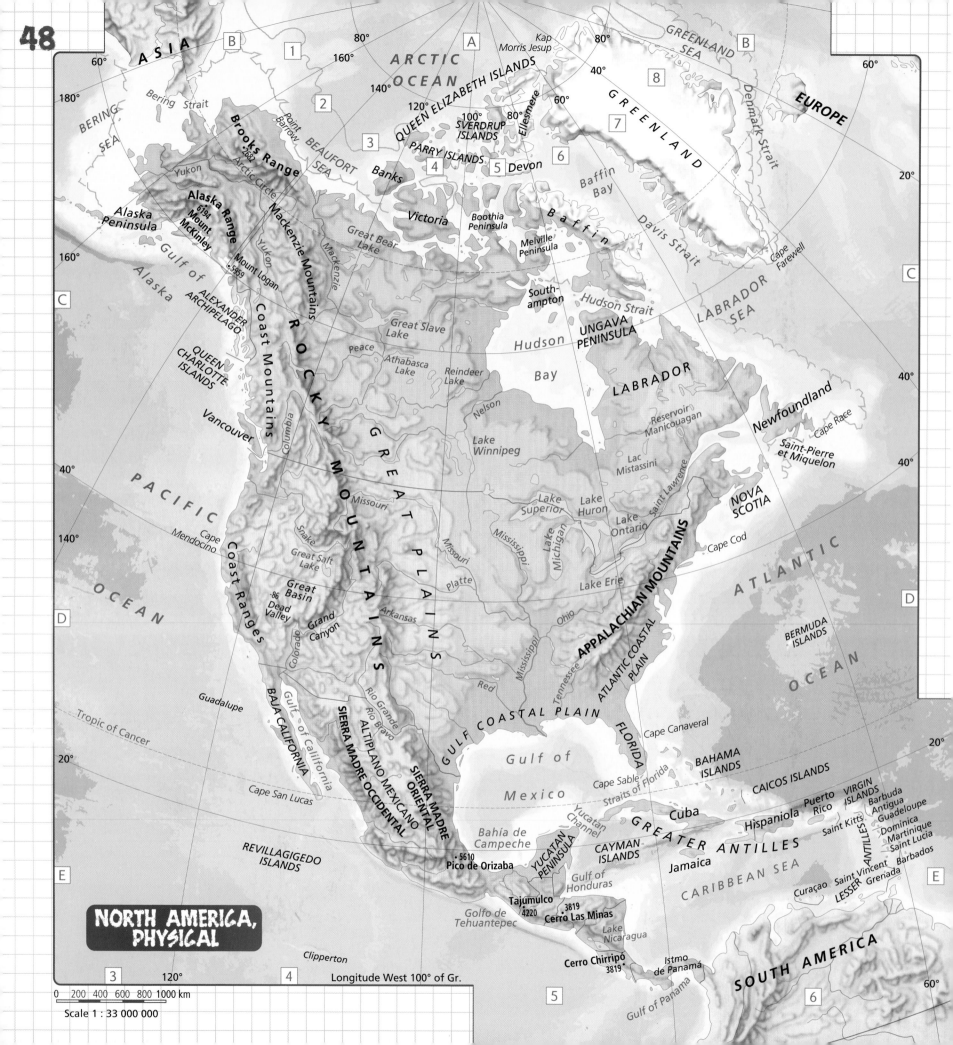

NORTH AMERICA, PHYSICAL

48

ASIA

ARCTIC OCEAN

BERING SEA

Bering Strait

Point Barrow

BEAUFORT SEA

Kap Morris Jesup

GREENLAND SEA

EUROPE

QUEEN ELIZABETH ISLANDS

SVERDRUP ISLANDS

PARRY ISLANDS

Ellesmere

GREENLAND

Denmark Strait

Banks

Devon

Victoria

Boothia Peninsula

Baffin

Melville Peninsula

Baffin Bay

Davis Strait

Cape Farewell

Brooks Range
.2682

Yukon

Arctic Circle

Mackenzie Mountains

Alaska Peninsula

Alaska Range
6194
Mount McKinley

Mount Logan
.5959

Yukon

Great Bear Lake

South-ampton

Hudson Strait

LABRADOR SEA

Alaska

Gulf of Alaska

ALEXANDER ARCHIPELAGO

Mackenzie

Great Slave Lake

UNGAVA PENINSULA

QUEEN CHARLOTTE ISLANDS

Coast Mountains

peace

Athabasca Lake

Reindeer Lake

Hudson Bay

LABRADOR

Vancouver

ROCKY MOUNTAINS

Columbia

GREAT PLAINS

Nelson

Lake Winnipeg

Reservoir Manicouagan

Newfoundland

Cape Race

Saint-Pierre et Miquelon

PACIFIC OCEAN

Cape Mendocino

Snake

Missouri

Lake Superior

Lake Huron

Saint Lawrence

Lac Mistassini

NOVA SCOTIA

Great Salt Lake

Great Basin

-86 Dead Valley

Colorado

Grand Canyon

Arkansas

Missouri

Mississippi

Lake Michigan

Lake Ontario

Lake Erie

APPALACHIAN MOUNTAINS

Cape Cod

ATLANTIC

BERMUDA ISLANDS

Platte

Ohio

Tennessee

ATLANTIC COASTAL PLAIN

OCEAN

Coast Ranges

Guadalupe

Tropic of Cancer

Rio Grande

Rio Bravo

Red

Mississippi

GULF COASTAL PLAIN

FLORIDA

Cape Canaveral

BAJA CALIFORNIA

Gulf of California

ALTIPLANO MEXICANO

SIERRA MADRE OCCIDENTAL

SIERRA MADRE ORIENTAL

Cape Sable

Straits of Florida

BAHAMA ISLANDS

CAICOS ISLANDS

Cape San Lucas

Gulf of Mexico

Yucatan Channel

Cuba

Hispaniola

Puerto Rico

VIRGIN ISLANDS

Barbuda

Antigua

REVILLAGIGEDO ISLANDS

Bahía de Campeche

YUCATAN PENINSULA

CAYMAN ISLANDS

GREATER ANTILLES

Saint Kitts

Guadeloupe

Dominica

Martinique

Saint Lucia

Pico de Orizaba
· 5610

Jamaica

CARIBBEAN SEA

Curaçao

Saint Vincent

LESSER

Barbados

Grenada

ANTILLES

Gulf of Honduras

Clipperton

Tajumulco
3819

Cerro Las Minas
3819
4220

Golfo de Tehuantepec

Lake Nicaragua

Cerro Chirripó
3819·

Istmo de Panamá

Gulf of Panama

SOUTH AMERICA

Longitude West 100° of Gr.

0 200 400 600 800 1000 km

Scale 1 : 33 000 000

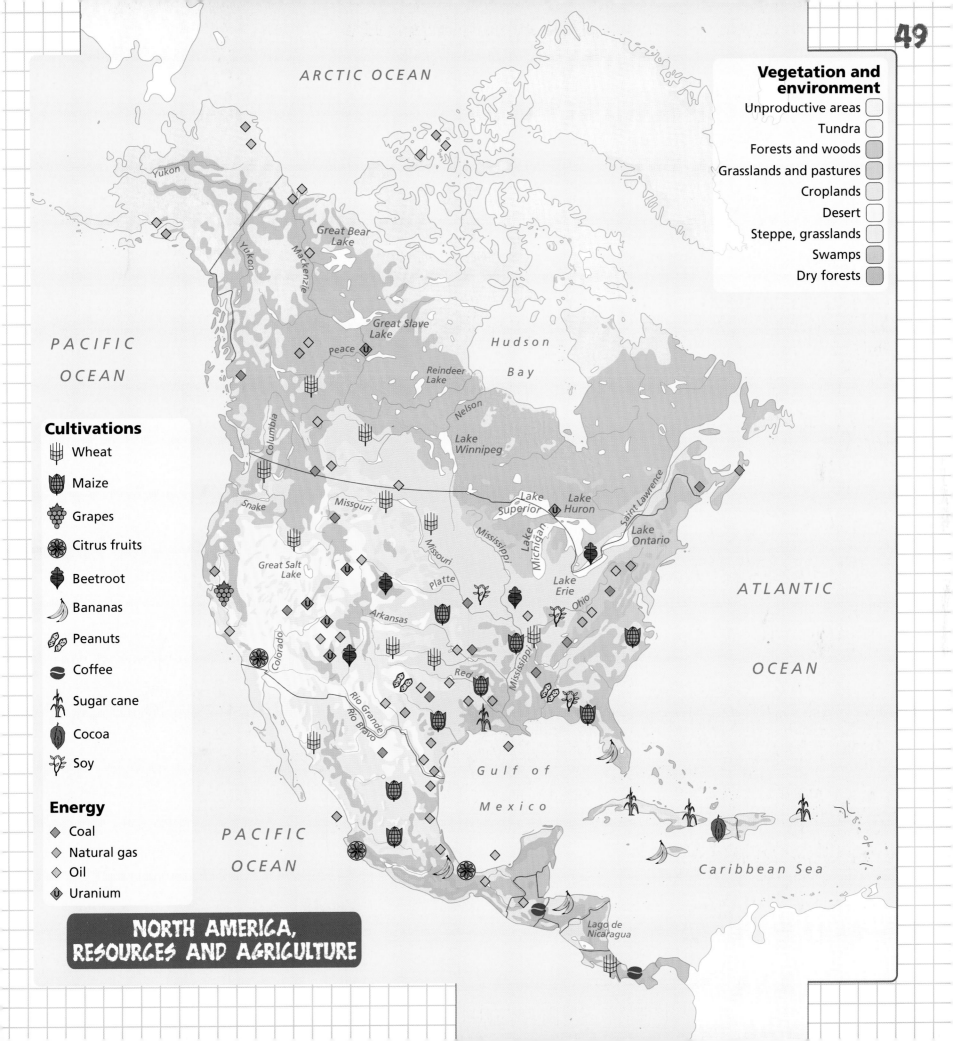

Vegetation and environment

- Unproductive areas
- Tundra
- Forests and woods
- Grasslands and pastures
- Croplands
- Desert
- Steppe, grasslands
- Swamps
- Dry forests

Cultivations

- 🌾 Wheat
- Maize
- 🍇 Grapes
- Citrus fruits
- Beetroot
- 🍌 Bananas
- Peanuts
- Coffee
- Sugar cane
- Cocoa
- Soy

Energy

- ◆ Coal
- ◇ Natural gas
- ◇ Oil
- ⚛ Uranium

ARCTIC OCEAN

PACIFIC OCEAN

Yukon

Great Bear Lake

Mackenzie

Yukon

Great Slave Lake

peace

Reindeer Lake

Hudson Bay

Nelson

Lake Winnipeg

Columbia

Snake

Missouri

Great Salt Lake

Missouri

Lake Superior

Lake Michigan

Lake Huron

Saint Lawrence

Lake Ontario

Lake Erie

Ohio

Mississippi

Platte

Arkansas

ATLANTIC OCEAN

Colorado

Rio Grande

Rio Bravo

Red

Mississippi

Gulf of Mexico

PACIFIC OCEAN

Caribbean Sea

Lago de Nicaragua

NORTH AMERICA, RESOURCES AND AGRICULTURE

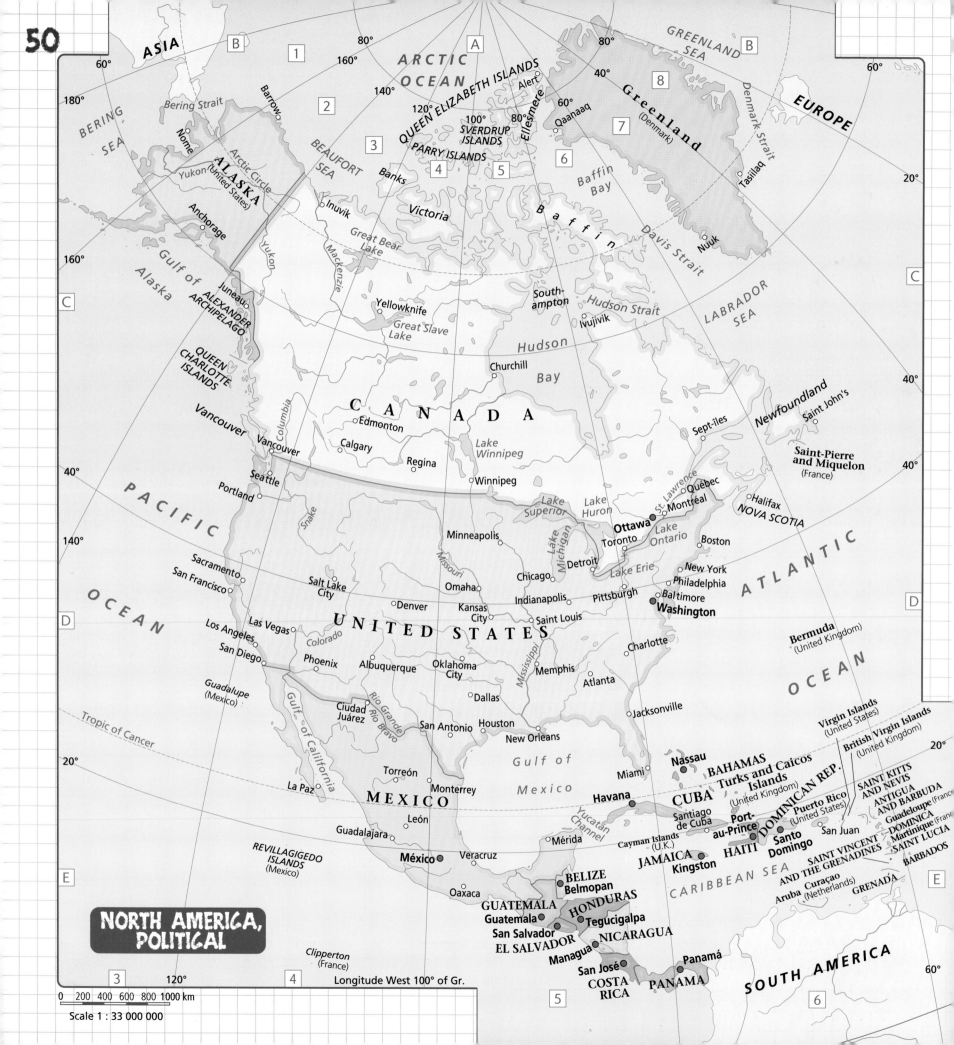

50

NORTH AMERICA, POLITICAL

Scale 1 : 33 000 000

0 200 400 600 800 1000 km

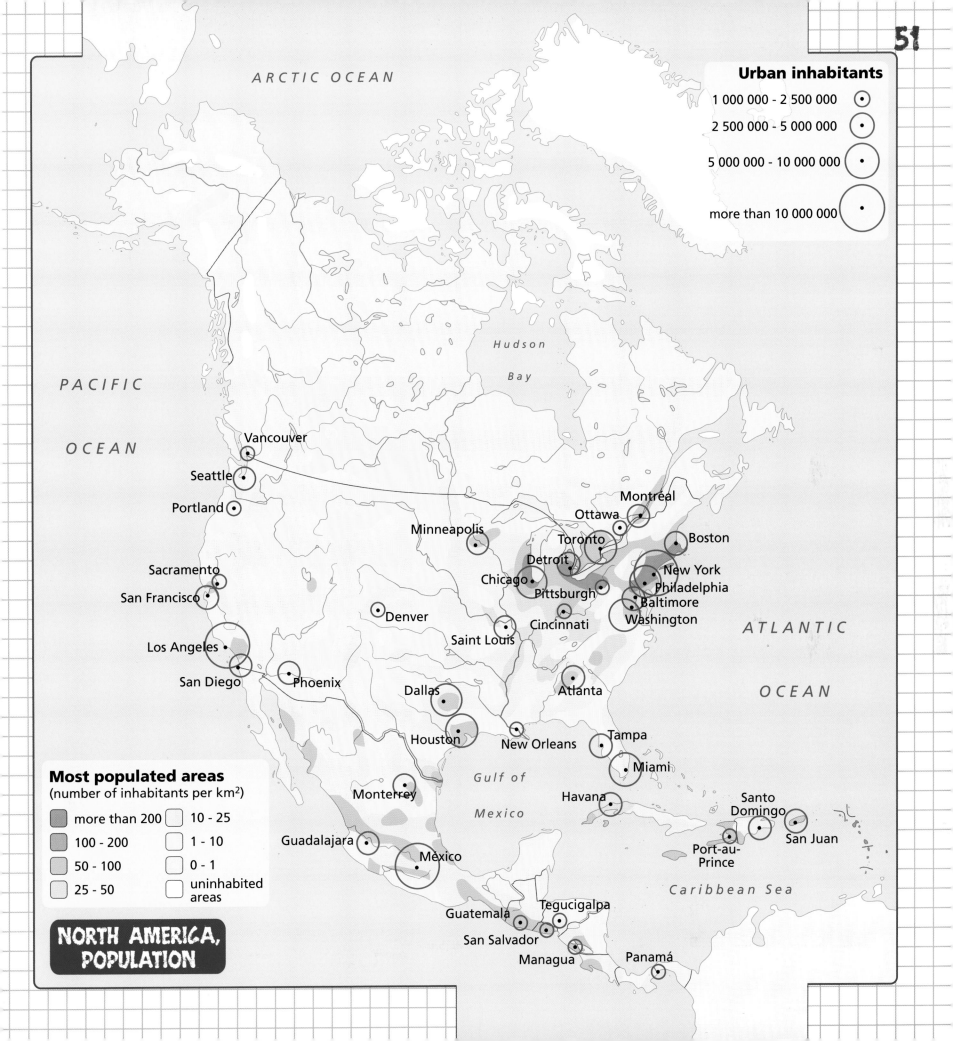

ARCTIC OCEAN

51

Urban inhabitants

1 000 000 - 2 500 000
2 500 000 - 5 000 000
5 000 000 - 10 000 000
more than 10 000 000

PACIFIC

OCEAN

Hudson

Bay

Vancouver
Seattle
Portland
Minneapolis
Montréal
Ottawa
Toronto
Boston
Detroit
New York
Sacramento
Chicago
Pittsburgh
Philadelphia
San Francisco
Baltimore
Washington
ATLANTIC
Denver
Cincinnati
Los Angeles
Saint Louis
OCEAN
San Diego
Phoenix
Atlanta
Dallas
Houston
Tampa
New Orleans
Miami

Gulf of

Monterrey
Havana
Santo
Domingo
San Juan

Most populated areas
(number of inhabitants per km²)

more than 200 | 10 - 25
100 - 200 | 1 - 10
50 - 100 | 0 - 1
25 - 50 | uninhabited areas

Guadalajara
México

Mexico

Port-au-
Prince

Caribbean Sea

NORTH AMERICA, POPULATION

Guatemala
Tegucigalpa
San Salvador
Managua
Panamá

52

...DID YOU KNOW THAT...

It's now a fact. Christopher Columbus wasn't the first European to land on the American coasts. It's a fact that he was beaten there by Viking navigators, who arrived on the island of Newfoundland at least 400 years before. It is testified by the remains of a Viking village discovered in 1960 by two Norwegian archaeologists.

Greenland

Alaska
2

1

2

4

5 7 8 2 9 10 12

3 11 13 14

6 15

17
16 19
18 20 22
21

NORTH AMERICAN COUNTRIES

CANADA
Capital: Ottawa
Population: 33 311 000

UNITED STATES (U.S.)
Capital: Washington, D.C.
Population: 304 060 000

MEXICO
Capital: México City
Population: 106 700 000

BAHAMAS
Capital: Nassau
Population: 86 000

CUBA
Capital: Havana
Population: 11 237 000

JAMAICA
Capital: Kingston
Population: 2 686 816

HAITI
Capital: Port-au-Prince
Population: 9 300 000

DOMINICAN REPUBLIC
Capital: Santo Domingo
Population: 9 407 000

ANTIGUA AND BARBUDA
Capital: Saint John's
Population: 86 000

SAINT KITTS AND NEVIS
Capital: Basseterre
Population: 41 000

SAINT LUCIA
Capital: Castries
Population: 171 000

DOMINICA
Capital: Roseau
Population: 70 000

GEO...QUIZ!

1. To the north of Canada there's an island, now belonging to Denmark, which could become independent in a few years. Which is it?

A Ellesmere   B Victoria   C Greenland

2. New York is the most populated city in the USA. But it isn't its capital, which is instead named after the country's first president. What's its name?

A Jackson   B Washington   C Lincoln

3. In 1920 an artificial canal was opened, which connected the Atlantic Ocean with the Pacific Ocean. Do you know what it's called?

A Panama   B Suez   C Grand Canal

4. Between North and South America there's a sea that was infested with pirates 400 years ago. Do you remember its name?

A Bering   B Labrador   C Caribbean

...FUN FACT...

The Mayan civilisation was already practically extinct when the Spanish arrived in America in the sixteenth century. We still don't know the reason for this, but the farming techniques of the Maya were probably not sufficiently developed to feed the constantly growing population. This caused famine and, consequently, wars and migration. The Spanish Conquistadores found virtually no resistance during the conquest until they encountered the Aztec and Inca peoples, whom they exterminated without mercy.

Yellowstone National Park is located in the north-west of the USA and is the oldest park in the world. It was in fact founded in 1872. It protects a wide variety of animals including grizzly bears, wolves, bison and moose. The park is also famous for its wealth of hot springs and geysers, whose jets of boiling water exceed 50 metres in height. These phenomena occur as Yellowstone (so-called due to the colour of sulphur) stands on a gigantic, underground supervolcano that will erupt sooner or later.

13

ST. VICENT AND THE GRENADINES
Capital: Kingstown
Population: 104 000

14

BARBADOS
Capital: Bridgetown
Population: 275 000

15

GRENADA
Capital: Saint George's
Population: 106 000

16

GUATEMALA
Capital: Guatemala City
Population: 13 697 000

17

BELIZE
Capital: Belmopan
Population: 322 100

18

EL SALVADOR
Capital: San Salvador
Population: 5 825 000

19

HONDURAS
Capital: Tegucigalpa
Population: 7 707 000

20

NICARAGUA
Capital: Managua
Population: 5 405 000

21

COSTA RICA
Capital: San José
Population: 4 382 000

22

PANAMA
Capital: Panama City
Population: 3 396 000

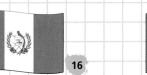

54

NORTH AMERICA

CARIBBEAN SEA

Punta Gallinas
Aruba
Trinidad

ATLANTIC

OCEAN

AFRICA

Lake Maracaibo
Pico Bolívar •5007
Sierra Nevada del Cocuy 5493

L L A N O S

Orinoco

Angel Falls

GUAIANA HIGHLANDS

2875 Mount Roraima

Mouth of Amazon

Equator

Isla del Coco

Isla de Malpelo

Chimborazo 6310

0°

Putumayo
Japurá

Río Negro
Amazon

Tapajós

Xingu

Tocantins

Parnaíba

Fernando de Noronha

Cape San Roque

GALAPAGOS ISLANDS

Punta Pariñas

Marañón

Ucayali

Juruá

Purus

Madeira

S E L V A S

Tocantins

Araguaia

Represa de Sobradinho

Huascarán 6768

Lake Titicaca

Guaporé

PLATEAU OF MATO GROSSO

São Francisco

BRAZILIAN HIGHLANDS

PACIFIC

Nevado Coropuna 6305

Nevado de Illimani 6402

Paraguay

ALTIPLANO

2890

Trindade

MARTIM VAZ ISLANDS

Gulf of Arica

20°

A N D E S

GRAN CHACO

Paraná

C A M P O S

Cabo Frio

Tropic of Capricorn

OCEAN

DESVENTURADAS ISLANDS

Nevado Ojos del Salado 6893

Salado

Uruguay

S E R R A   D O   M A R

ATLANTIC

JUAN FERNÁNDEZ ISLANDS

Aconcagua 6959

P A M P A S

Paraná

Patos Lagoon

Río de la Plata

OCEAN

Colorado

Chiloé Island

40 Península Valdés

Gulf of San Jorge
Cape Tres Puntas

C O R D I L L E R A   P A T A G Ó N I C A
P A T A G O N I A

4058

FALKLAND ISLANDS

South Georgia

Tierra del Fuego

Strait of Magellan

Cape Horn

SOUTH AMERICA, PHYSICAL

0 200 400 600 800 1000 km
Scale 1 : 33 000 000

ATLANTIC

OCEAN

Caribbean Sea

Lago de
Maracaibo

Orinoco

Meta

Putumayo

Japurá

Rio Negro

Amazon

Jari

Marañón

Juruá

Purus

Madeira

Tapajós

Xingu

Tocantins

Parnaíba

Tocantins

Araguaia

Represa de
Sobradinho

São Francisco

Lake
Titicaca

Guaporé

PACIFIC

OCEAN

Paraguay

Paraná

Pilcomayo

Salado

Uruguay

Parana

Colorado

ATLANTIC

OCEAN

Vegetation and environment

Unproductive areas

Forests and woods

Grasslands and pastures

Croplands

Desert

Swamps

Dry forests

Savannah

Cultivations

Wheat

Maize

Rice

Grapes

Citrus fruits

Bananas

Coffee

Sugar cane

Tea

Cocoa

Soy

Energy

◇ Coal

◇ Natural gas

◇ Oil

⚛ Uranium

SOUTH AMERICA, RESOURCES AND AGRICULTURE

20°

NORTH AMERICA

CARIBBEAN SEA

AFRICA

(Netherlands)
Aruba Curaçao

Barranquilla Maracaibo

Port of Spain

**TRINIDAD
AND TOBAGO**

Caracas

A

A T L A N T I C

Medellín

Orinoco Ciudad
Guayana

Georgetown

SURINAME **Paramaribo**

O C E A N

COLOMBIA

VENEZUELA

G U Y A N A

Cayenne

Cali

Bogotá

**French
Guiana**

Boa Vista

Macapá

*Isla del Coco
(Costa Rica)*

*Isla de Malpelo
(Colombia)*

Equator

Quito

ECUADOR

Rio Negro

Amazon

Belém

0°

**GALAPAGOS
ISLANDS
(Ecuador)**

Guayaquil

Putumayo

Japurá

Mánaus

Tapajós

Fortaleza

*Fernando
de Noronha
(Brazil)*

Iquitos

Marañón

Teresina

Ucayali

Purus

Madeira

Xingu

B R A Z I L

Trujillo

Rio
Branco

Porto Velho

Recife

PERU

Tocantins

B

Lima

PACIFIC

Cusco

*Lake
Titicaca*

Cuiabá

Brasília

São Francisco

Salvador

Arequipa

La Paz

BOLIVIA

Goiânia

Montes Claros

Arica

Sucre

Paraguay

Belo Horizonte

Campo Grande

*Trindade
(Brazil)*

20°

Tropic of Capricorn

Antofagasta

Pilcomayo

PARAGUAY

Salta

São Paulo

Rio de Janeiro

*MARTIM VAZ
ISLANDS
(Brazil)*

O C E A N

*DESVENTURADAS
ISLANDS
(Chile)*

CHILE

Asunción

Paraná

Santos

Curitiba

Corrientes

Porto Alegre

*JUAN FERNÁNDEZ
ISLANDS
(Chile)*

Córdoba

Uruguay

Paraná

URUGUAY

Valparaíso

Santiago

Buenos Aires

Montevideo

C

A T L A N T I C

Concepción

ARGENTINA

Río de la Plata

Bahía Blanca

O C E A N

Puerto Montt

*Chiloé
Island*

Comodoro
Rivadavia

40°

**SOUTH AMERICA,
POLITICAL**

Wellington

Falkland Islands
(United Kingdom)*

D

*Strait of
Magellan*

SOUTH GEORGIA
(United Kingdom)*

* Islands claimed by Argentina

Punta Arenas

*Tierra
del Fuego*

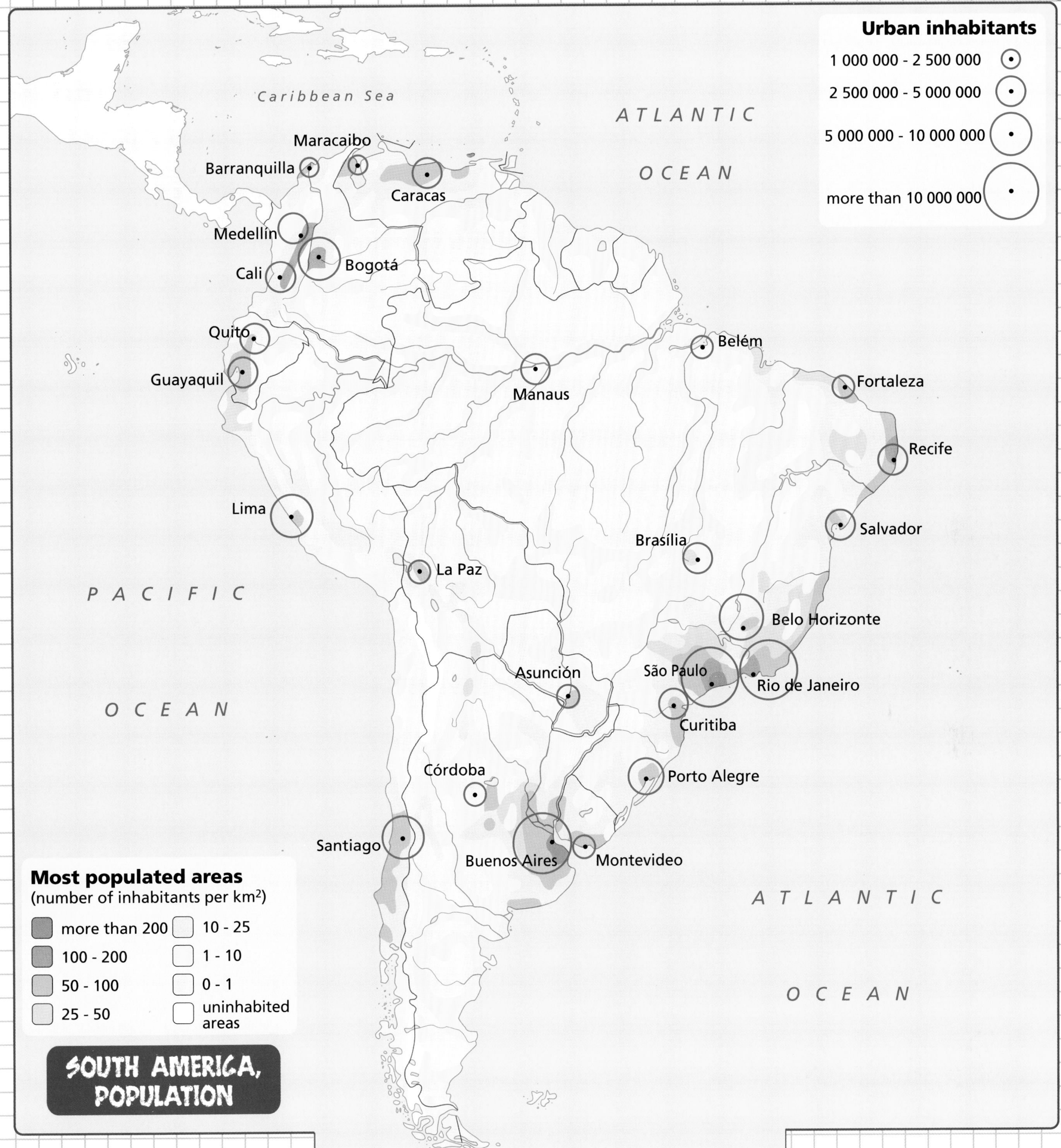

Urban inhabitants

1 000 000 - 2 500 000	⊙
2 500 000 - 5 000 000	⊙
5 000 000 - 10 000 000	⊙
more than 10 000 000	⊙

Caribbean Sea

ATLANTIC

OCEAN

Maracaibo

Barranquilla

Caracas

Medellín

Cali

Bogotá

Quito

Guayaquil

Belém

Fortaleza

Manaus

Recife

Lima

Salvador

Brasília

PACIFIC

La Paz

Belo Horizonte

OCEAN

Asunción

São Paulo

Rio de Janeiro

Curitiba

Córdoba

Porto Alegre

Santiago

Buenos Aires

Montevideo

ATLANTIC

OCEAN

Most populated areas
(number of inhabitants per km²)

▓ more than 200		░ 10 - 25	
▓ 100 - 200		░ 1 - 10	
▒ 50 - 100		░ 0 - 1	
░ 25 - 50		▫ uninhabited areas	

SOUTH AMERICA, POPULATION

...DID YOU KNOW THAT...

The Galapagos Islands are a paradise for all nature lovers. They rise up 1000 kilometres to the west of the coast of Ecuador. Due to their isolation, they have become a natural laboratory in which plants and animals have evolved as if in a world of their own.

The great naturalist Charles Darwin landed there in 1835 and he understood the mechanism of natural evolution by studying the flora and fauna. The giant tortoises are symbolic of the islands. Some specimens reach 2 metres in length, they weigh 250 kilos and are over 100 years old.

SOUTH AMERICAN COUNTRIES

French Guiana

...FUN FACT...

In the Andes, man has adapted to live and work at very high altitudes. Clear examples of this are the Bolivian city of La Paz, situated at 3627 metres above sea level and the Peruvian Lima-La Oroya railway, which reaches 4829 metres above sea level.

Given that the main problem is the drop in breathable oxygen, the people of the Andes have more efficient lungs and a type of blood capable of transporting more oxygen to the muscles and brain.

GEO...QUIZ!

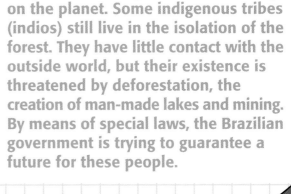

1. The Atacama Desert is regarded as the most arid point on Earth. It is said that it hasn't rained there for 400 years! In which country is it found?

A Argentina   B Chile   C Bolivia

2. The Amazon river pours enough fresh water back into the sea to replenish the whole of the US for five months. Which ocean does it flow into?

A Atlantic   B Pacific   C Indian

3. In South America there's still a colony, French Guiana, whose capital is sadly famous for having been home to a terrible prison. What's it called?

A Paramaribo   B Georgetown   C Cayenne

4. The highest waterfall in the world is found in Venezuela. Its drop reaches 979 metres. What's its name?

A Angel Falls   B Iguassu   C Niagara

...FUN FACT...

The great Amazon rainforest (Selvas) is home to over 3 million plant and animal species, which is why it is regarded as the place with the greatest "biodiversity" on the planet. Some indigenous tribes (indios) still live in the isolation of the forest. They have little contact with the outside world, but their existence is threatened by deforestation, the creation of man-made lakes and mining. By means of special laws, the Brazilian government is trying to guarantee a future for these people.

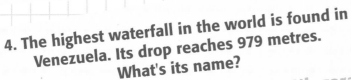

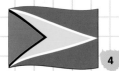 **1**
COLOMBIA
Capital: Bogotá
Population: 39 746 000

VENEZUELA **2**
Capital: Caracas
Population: 28 384 320

 **3**
TRINIDAD AND TOBAGO
Capital: Port of Spain
Population: 1 310 000

 **4**
GUYANA
Capital: Georgetown
Population: 766 000

 **5**
SURINAME
Capital: Paramaribo
Population: 513 000

 **6**
ECUADOR
Capital: Quito
Population: 13 805 000

 **7**
PERU
Capital: Lima
Population: 28 221 000

 **8**
BRAZIL
Capital: Brasília
Population: 186 560 000

 **9**
CHILE
Capital: Santiago
Population: 16 763 000

 **10**
BOLIVIA
Capital: Sucre, La Paz
Population: 10 028 000

 **11**
PARAGUAY
Capital: Asunción
Population: 6 230 000

 **12**
ARGENTINA
Capital: Buenos Aires
Population: 39 746 000

 **13**
URUGUAY
Capital: Montevideo
Population: 3 334 000

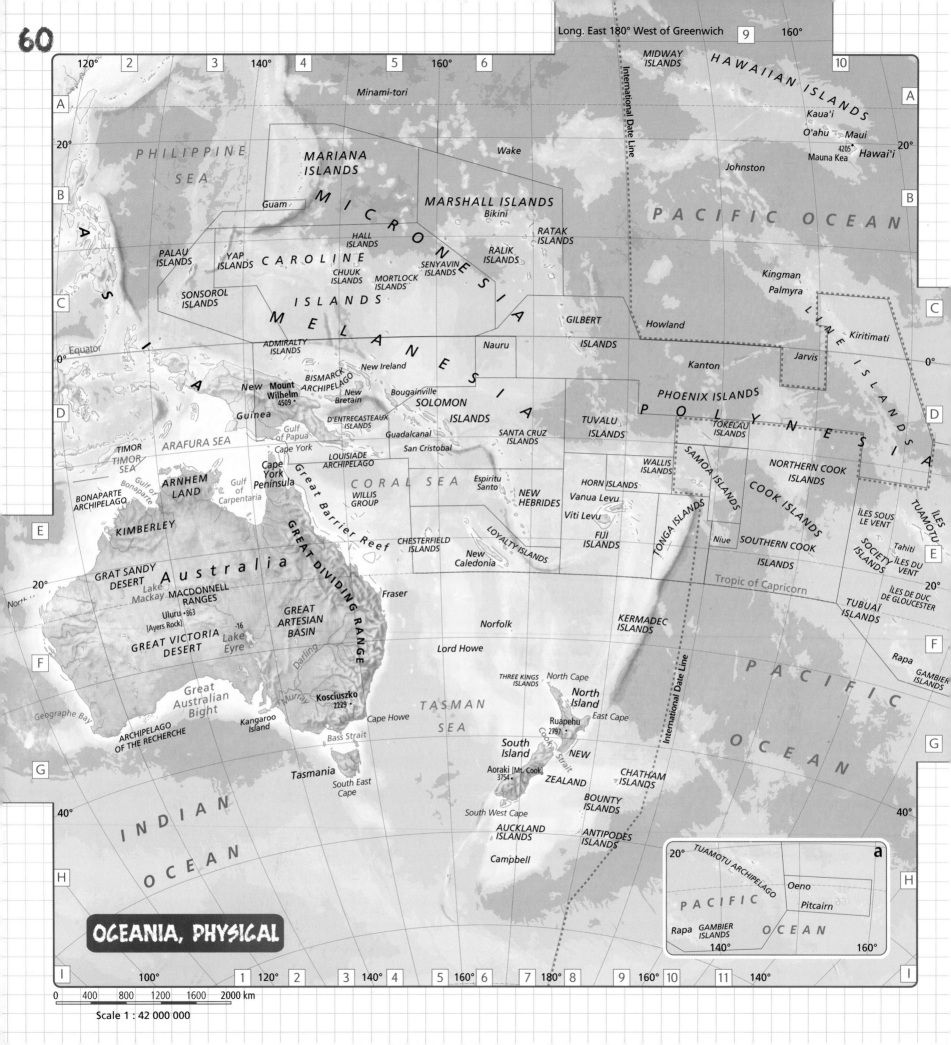

60

120° 2 3 140° 4 160° 5 160° 6

MIDWAY ISLANDS

HAWAIIAN ISLANDS 10

A

Minami-tori

Kaua'i
O'ahu Maui
4205
Mauna Kea Hawai'i

20°

Wake

Johnston

20°

PHILIPPINE

MARIANA ISLANDS

MICRONESIA

MARSHALL ISLANDS

PACIFIC OCEAN

B

SEA

Guam

Bikini

RATAK ISLANDS

PALAU ISLANDS

YAP ISLANDS

CAROLINE

HALL ISLANDS

RALIK ISLANDS

Kingman
Palmyra

C

SONSOROL ISLANDS

CHUUK ISLANDS

MORTLOCK ISLANDS

SENYAVIN ISLANDS

ISLANDS

MELANESIA

GILBERT

Howland

LINE ISLANDS

Kiritimati

Jarvis

ADMIRALTY ISLANDS

Nauru

ISLANDS

0°

Equator 0°

Kanton

New Ireland

BISMARCK ARCHIPELAGO

New Britain

Bougainville

SOLOMON ISLANDS

POLYNESIA

PHOENIX ISLANDS

D

New
Mount Wilhelm 4509

Guinea

D'ENTRECASTEAUX ISLANDS

TUVALU ISLANDS

TOKELAU ISLANDS

Gulf of Papua

Guadalcanal

SANTA CRUZ ISLANDS

San Cristobal

WALLIS ISLANDS

NORTHERN COOK ISLANDS

ÎLES TUAMOTU

ARAFURA SEA

Cape York

LOUISIADE ARCHIPELAGO

CORAL SEA

SAMOA ISLANDS

E

TIMOR TIMOR SEA

ARNHEM LAND

Gulf of Carpentaria

Cape York

WILLIS GROUP

Espiritu Santo

HORN ISLANDS

COOK ISLANDS

ÎLES SOUS LE VENT

BONAPARTE ARCHIPELAGO

Bonaparte

Peninsula

Great Barrier Reef

CHESTERFIELD ISLANDS

NEW HEBRIDES

Vanua Levu

Niue

SOUTHERN COOK

Tahiti

SOCIETY ISLANDS

ÎLES DU VENT

KIMBERLEY

GREAT DIVIDING RANGE

Viti Levu

FIJI ISLANDS

ISLANDS

ÎLES DE DUC DE GLOUCESTER

F

North

GRAT SANDY DESERT

Australia

Lake Mackay

MACDONNELL RANGES

LOYALTY ISLANDS

New Caledonia

TONGA ISLANDS

Tropic of Capricorn

TUBUAI ISLANDS

20°

Uluru •863 [Ayers Rock]

-16

GREAT ARTESIAN BASIN

Fraser

20°

Rapa

GAMBIER ISLANDS

GREAT VICTORIA DESERT

Lake Eyre

Darling

Norfolk

KERMADEC ISLANDS

Lord Howe

THREE KINGS ISLANDS

North Cape

PACIFIC

G

Great Australian Bight

Murray

Kosciuszko 2229

TASMAN SEA

North Island

Ruapehu 2797

East Cape

Geographe Bay

Kangaroo Island

Cape Howe

Cook Strait

NEW

ARCHIPELAGO OF THE RECHERCHE

Bass Strait

South Island

Aoraki [Mt. Cook] 3754

ZEALAND

CHATHAM ISLANDS

OCEAN

G

Tasmania

South East Cape

BOUNTY ISLANDS

INDIAN

South West Cape

H

OCEAN

AUCKLAND ISLANDS

ANTIPODES ISLANDS

Campbell

40° 40°

OCEANIA, PHYSICAL

20° TUAMOTU ARCHIPELAGO

a

Oeno

PACIFIC

Pitcairn

Rapa GAMBIER ISLANDS

OCEAN

140° 160°

I

100° 1 120° 2 3 140° 4 160° 5 6 180° 7 8 160° 9 10 11 140° I

International Date Line

0 400 800 1200 1600 2000 km

Scale 1 : 42 000 000

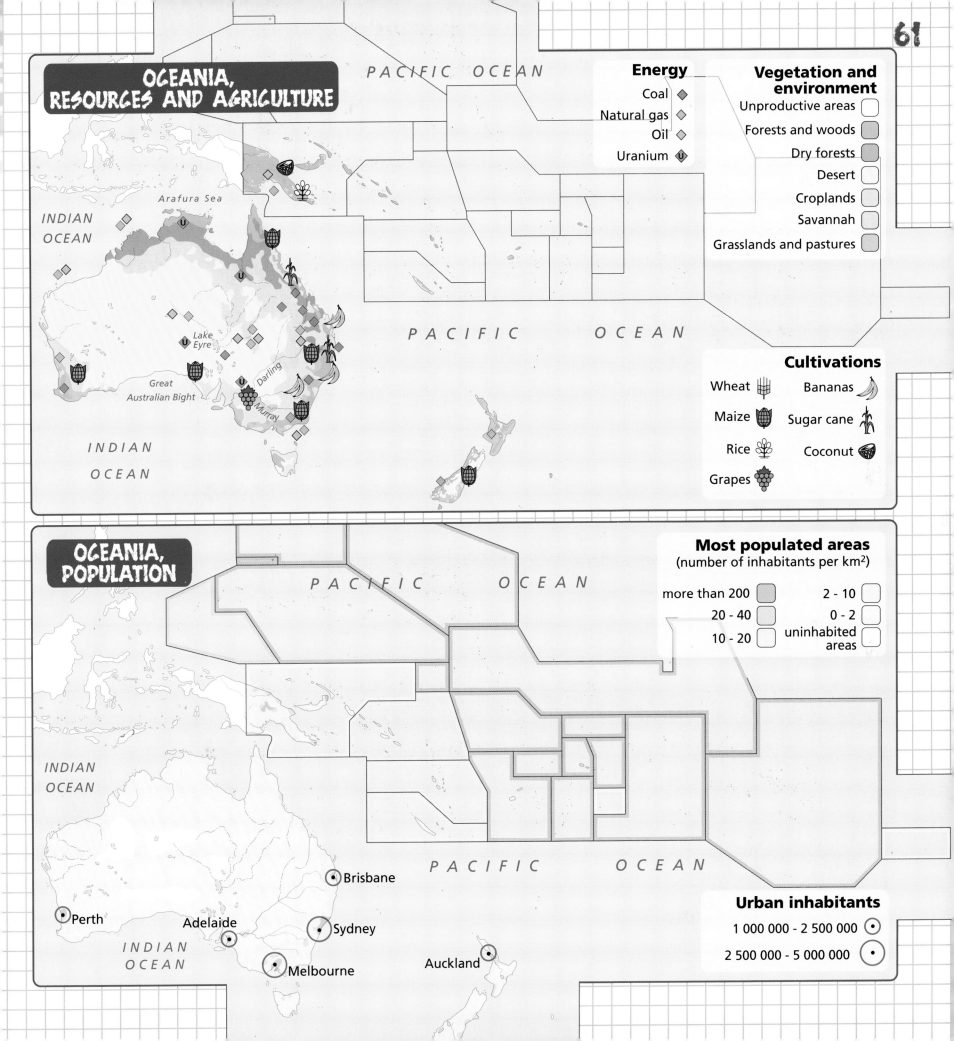

OCEANIA, RESOURCES AND AGRICULTURE

PACIFIC OCEAN

Arafura Sea

INDIAN OCEAN

INDIAN OCEAN

Lake Eyre

Great Australian Bight

Darling

Murray

Energy

Coal ◆
Natural gas ◆
Oil ◆
Uranium Ⓤ

Vegetation and environment

Unproductive areas
Forests and woods
Dry forests
Desert
Croplands
Savannah
Grasslands and pastures

Cultivations

Wheat
Maize
Rice
Grapes

Bananas
Sugar cane
Coconut

OCEANIA, POPULATION

PACIFIC OCEAN

INDIAN OCEAN

PACIFIC OCEAN

INDIAN OCEAN

Brisbane

Perth

Adelaide

Sydney

Melbourne

Auckland

Most populated areas
(number of inhabitants per km²)

more than 200
20 - 40
10 - 20

2 - 10
0 - 2
uninhabited areas

Urban inhabitants

1 000 000 - 2 500 000 ⊙
2 500 000 - 5 000 000 ⊙

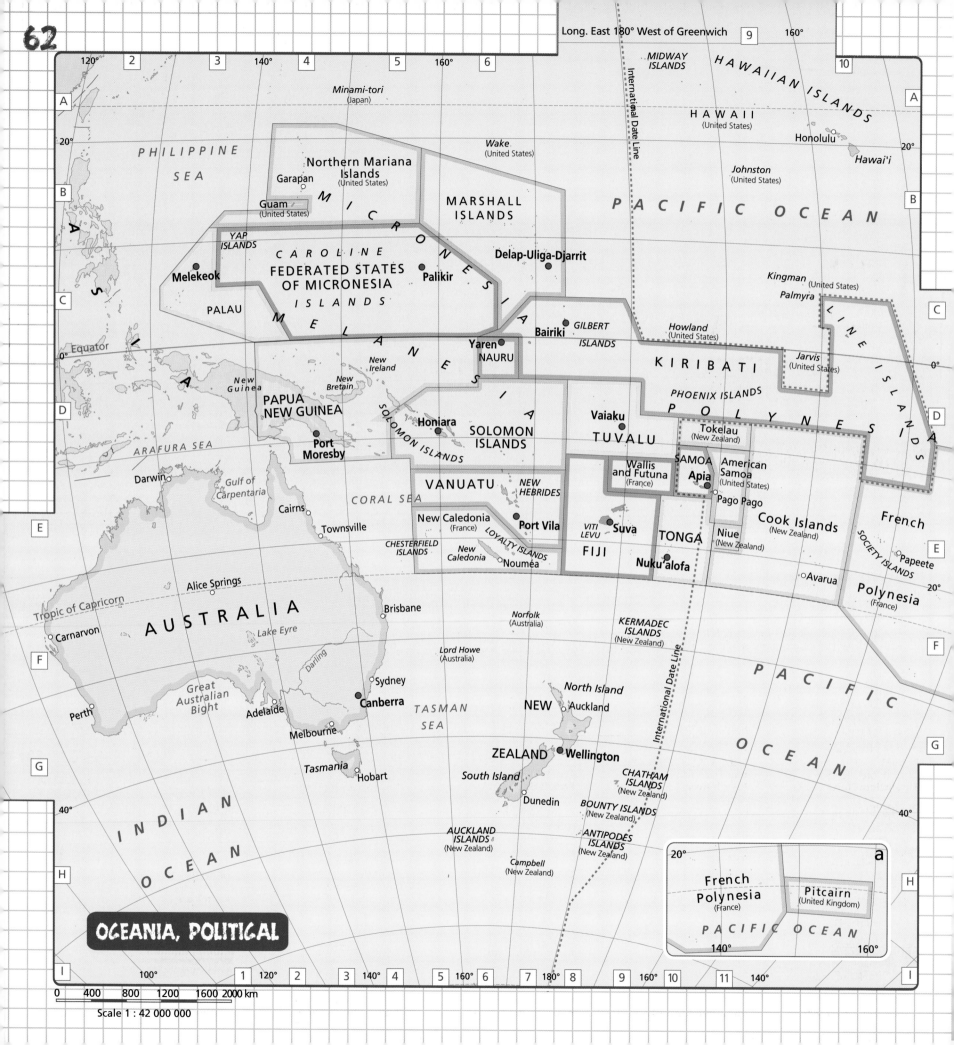

62

MIDWAY ISLANDS

HAWAIIAN ISLANDS

PHILIPPINE SEA

Minami-tori (Japan)

Wake (United States)

HAWAII (United States)

PACIFIC OCEAN

Honolulu

Hawai'i

Northern Mariana Islands (United States)

Garapan

Guam (United States)

MARSHALL ISLANDS

Johnston (United States)

MICRONESIA

YAP ISLANDS

CAROLINE

Melekeok

FEDERATED STATES OF MICRONESIA

Palikir

ISLANDS

Delap-Uliga-Djarrit

Kingman (United States)

Palmyra

MELANESIA

PALAU

LINE ISLANDS

Equator

0°

Bairiki

GILBERT ISLANDS

Howland (United States)

KIRIBATI

Jarvis (United States)

0°

Yaren
NAURU

POLYNESIA

New Ireland

New Guinea

New Bretain

PHOENIX ISLANDS

PAPUA NEW GUINEA

SOLOMON ISLANDS

Honiara

SOLOMON ISLANDS

Vaiaku

TUVALU

Tokelau (New Zealand)

SAMOA

American Samoa (United States)

ARAFURA SEA

Port Moresby

Wallis and Futuna (France)

Apia

French

Darwin

Gulf of Carpentaria

VANUATU

NEW HEBRIDES

Pago Pago

Cairns

CORAL SEA

SOCIETY ISLANDS

Townsville

New Caledonia (France)

Port Vila

VITI LEVU

Suva

TONGA

Niue (New Zealand)

Cook Islands (New Zealand)

Papeete

CHESTERFIELD ISLANDS

New Caledonia

LOYALTY ISLANDS

FIJI

Nuku'alofa

Polynesia (France)

Tropic of Capricorn

Nouméa

Avarua

20°

Alice Springs

AUSTRALIA

Brisbane

Norfolk (Australia)

KERMADEC ISLANDS (New Zealand)

Carnarvon

Lake Eyre

Lord Howe (Australia)

PACIFIC

Perth

Darling

Sydney

NEW

North Island

Auckland

Adelaide

Canberra

TASMAN SEA

OCEAN

Melbourne

ZEALAND

Wellington

Tasmania

Hobart

South Island

CHATHAM ISLANDS (New Zealand)

Dunedin

BOUNTY ISLANDS (New Zealand)

40°

INDIAN

AUCKLAND ISLANDS (New Zealand)

ANTIPODES ISLANDS (New Zealand)

OCEAN

Campbell (New Zealand)

20°

a

French Polynesia (France)

Pitcairn (United Kingdom)

OCEANIA, POLITICAL

PACIFIC OCEAN

140°

160°

0   400   800   1200   1600 2000 km

Scale 1 : 42 000 000

COUNTRIES OF OCEANIA

DEPENDENCIES AND COLONIES
a Pitcairn (United kigndom)
b New Caledonia (France)
c Wallis and Futuna (France)
d French Polynesia (France)
e Guam (United States)
f Midway Islands (United States)
g Northern Mariana Is. (United States)
h American Samoa (United States)
i Hawai'i (United States)

GEO...QUIZ!

1. There's a large island that is divided politically between Oceania and Asia. Which is it?
A New Guinea B Nauru
C Tasmania

2. The capital of New Zealand has the same name as an English general. What's it called?
A Canberra B Wellington
C Yaren

3. The Hawaiian Islands belong geographically to Oceania, but politically they are...
A Japanese   B English
C American

...DID YOU KNOW THAT...

The world's most famous monolith (meaning a single block of stone), Ayers Rock, is situated in the great desert plain in central Australia. It's an immense rock of red sandstone, which rises 348 metres and has a circumference of 8 kilometres. It is called Uluru by the Aborigines, for whom it is a sacred place.

PALAU
Capital: Melekeok
Population: 20 300

FED. STATES OF MICRONESIA
Capital: Palikir
Population: 108 000

MARSHALL ISLANDS
Capital: Delap Uliga-Djarrit
Population: 53240

PAPUA NEW GUINEA
Capital: Port Moresby
Population: 6 348 000

NAURU
Capital: Yaren
Population: 10 160

KIRIBATI
Capital: South Tarawa
Population: 97 000

SOLOMON ISLANDS
Capital: Honiara
Population: 507 000

TUVALU
Capital: Funafuti
Population: 10 500

SAMOA
Capital: Apia
Population: 189 000

AUSTRALIA
Capital: Canberra
Population: 21 372 000

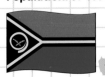

VANUATU
Capital: Port Vila
Population: 233 000

FIJI
Capital: Suva
Population: 844 000

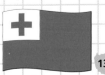

TONGA
Capital: Nuku'alofa
Population: 102 000

NEW ZEALAND
Capital: Wellington
Population: 4 269 000

64

PACIFIC OCEAN

150°   150°

Arctic Circle

Alaska
(United States)

Wrangel Island

120°   120°

CANADA

Banks   *S i b e r i a*   **ASIA**

NORTH AMERICA   ARCTIC   *NEW SIBERIAN ISLANDS*

Victoria

SEVERNAJA ZEMLJA

90°   90°

70°   80°   OCEAN   80°   70°   **RUSSIA**

Ellesmere
Nares Strait

Baffin

NOVAJA ZEMLJA

Greenland
(Denmark)   *SPITSBERGEN*
(Norway)   *Barents Sea*

60°   *Nordkapp*   60°

A T L A N T I C   *E U R O P E*

ICELAND   **NORWAY**   **FINLAND**

30°   **SWEDEN**   30°

OCEAN

Longitude West 0° East of Greenwich

...FUN FACT...

At the North Pole there's no surface land and the pack ice where the polar bears live is none other than the frozen water of the Arctic Ocean.
The pack ice covers about 15 million km² in the winter and 3.5 million km² in the summer, which is less than previous years due to global warming.
The Arctic therefore isn't a continent, but a combination of the sea and the northernmost lands of Asia, North America and Europe.

...DID YOU KNOW THAT...

Antarctica, which extends around the South Pole, is actually a continent in its own right, with a larger surface area than Europe. It measures approximately 14 000 000 km², of which 13 720 000 km² are covered with ice and 280 000 km² are free. It is the coldest continent on Earth and is home to various scientific stations where the climate and meteorology are studied.

POLES

0   500   1000   1500 km

Scale 1 : 50 000 000

ATLANTIC OCEAN

30°   30°

Antarctic Circle

SOUTH ORKNEY ISLANDS

60°   *Weddell Sea*   *Queen Maud Land*   *Enderby Land*   60°

Graham Land

Antarctic Peninsula   *Palmer Land*   *Coats Land*

Alexander Island   *Berkner*   *Amery Ice Shelf*

Ronne Ice Shelf   **ANTARCTICA**

Bellingshausen Sea   *Mount Vinson 4897*   South Pole

90°   70°   80°   *Transantarctic Mountains*   80°   70°   90°

Ellsworth Land   *Queen Mary Land*

Thurston

Amundsen Sea   *Marie Byrd Land*   *Ross Ice Shelf*   *Wilkes Land*

Roosevelt   3794 *Mount Erebus*

Ross Sea   *Victoria Land*   120°

Dumont D'Urville Sea

BALLENY ISLANDS
(New Zealand)

150°   150°

Longitude West 180° East of Greenwich   ○ scientific stations

INDEX OF NAMES

Solutions GEO...QUIZ!

EUROPE (page 29)
1. **B** Netherlands
2. **C** Pyrennes
3. **A** Berlin

EUROPE (page 31)
1. **B** North Cape
2. **A** Prague
3. **C** Black
4. **B** Montenegro

ASIA (page 37)
1. **B** Caspian
2. **A** Iraq
3. **C** Afghanistan
4. **B** Cyprus

ASIA (page 39)
1. **B** China
2. **A** Tōkyō
3. **C** Sri Lanka
4. **B** Singapore

AFRICA (page 45)
1. **C** Senegal
2. **C** Nile
3. **B** Mediterranean
4. **C** Rabat

AFRICA (page 47)
1. **C** a river
2. **B** Atlantic
3. **A** Madagascar
4. **C** Nairobi

NORTH AMERICA (page 53)
1. **C** Greenland
2. **B** Washington
3. **A** Panama
4. **C** Caribbean

SOUTH AMERICA (page 59)
1. **B** Chile
2. **A** Atlantic
3. **C** Cayenne
4. **A** Angel Falls

OCEANIA (page 63)
1. **A** New Guinea
2. **B** Wellington
3. **C** American